A Perfectly Imperfect Dad

The true story about a dad who lived through
the Great Depression and raised five sons
with common sense advice and large doses of humor.

Paul Kincaid

Copyright © 2017 Paul Kincaid.

Kincaid Communications, LLC
PO Box 2386, Springfield, MO 65801-2386
417-425-5139
www.KincaidCommunications.com

All rights reserved. No part of this book may be reproduced, stored, or transmitted by any means—whether auditory, graphic, mechanical, or electronic—without written permission of both publisher and author, except in the case of brief excerpts used in critical articles and reviews. Unauthorized reproduction of any part of this work is illegal and is punishable by law.

ISBN: 978-0-6927-8792-2 (sc)
ISBN: 978-1-5323-2310-2 (e)

Because of the dynamic nature of the Internet, any web addresses or links contained in this book may have changed since publication and may no longer be valid. The views expressed in this work are solely those of the author and do not necessarily reflect the views of the publisher, and the publisher hereby disclaims any responsibility for them.

Any people depicted in stock imagery provided by Thinkstock are models, and such images are being used for illustrative purposes only.
Certain stock imagery © Thinkstock.

Lulu Publishing Services rev. date: 03/07/2017

Contents

Acknowledgements vii

Introduction ix

Chapter One: A name and advice to live by 1

Chapter Two: Driving in the DNA 18

Chapter Three: Seventeen jobs, one career 35

Chapter Four: Embarrassing inspiration 58

Chapter Five: Game over 79

Dad's sincere thanks 93

Photos of Dad 103

About the author 117

Acknowledgements

Obviously, this book would not have been possible without the cooperation and blessing of Dad. The book is through my eyes, but his notes about his childhood and career were an invaluable resource. I also appreciated his willingness to talk about his life and to review an early draft of the first four chapters for accuracy. I hope I have captured his sense of humor and his success as a dad to his five sons. For him, being the best dad possible was the only goal that mattered.

There were many others who helped bring this book to life and I want to acknowledge them here.

- For the "perfectly imperfect" phrase used in the subtitle: Matt Kincaid

- For early reviews and feedback: Brian Kincaid, Jennifer Kincaid, Janet Kincaid, Jean Caldwell, Gary Snavely, Don Hendricks, and Laurie Phelan

- For helping check accuracy: Lance Kincaid, Eric Kincaid, Matt Kincaid, Susan Kincaid, and Jean Caldwell

- For final proofreading assistance: Stacey Funderburk and Jennifer Kincaid

- For marketing and website assistance: Don Hendricks and Jessica Clements

- For cover concept and design: Amy Schuldt

- For permission to use the photograph from which the cover photo was taken: Jesse Scheve

- For permission to use three interior photographs: Lynn Smith/Tintype Studio, Katie Day/Katie Day Photography, Lifetouch Inc. Photography for a Lifetime

- For permission to use the author photograph: Bob Linder

- For providing stories, family photos, and encouragement: Lots of family members

Introduction

My Dad, Everett Leon Kincaid, Jr. – E. Leon – was not perfect. Far from it.

For example, while he was careful not to curse when we were growing up – the strongest expression he used was, "oh, thunder" – he made up for it as he got older. He may have served in the Army National Guard, but he cussed like a sailor. When it came to politics, he was extremely conservative – slightly to the right of Attila the Hun, as the expression goes. Like many of his generation, he had strong, outdated ideas about race and sexual orientation. He would not have been mistaken for a feminist. He forwarded off-color and X-rated emails. He liked sending greeting cards that featured fart humor. You get the idea.

Dad wasn't perfect, but then again, he never claimed to be. He didn't have time. He was too busy trying to earn a living and be the best dad possible to his five sons – my four brothers and me. Those were his priorities, not perfection.

Growing up starting in the 1950s, until 1961 in Topeka, Kansas, and then in the suburbs of Kansas City, my four brothers and I were taught to treat people with respect. Beyond that, we admired many people: sports figures, especially baseball players; presidents; authors; and actors. We also admired coaches, teachers, and friends who influenced our lives.

But we only had one hero and we didn't have to look very far to find him.

He might be in the kitchen splattering grease as he made bacon and eggs for breakfast or fried several dozen tacos for dinner, two of his specialties. Or, he might be loading or unloading the dishwasher. He could be on the field coaching baseball or in the stands at one of our football games. Or, he could be lending an empathetic and supportive ear during a midnight visit in our teenage years. He could be traveling at all hours to make it back from a business trip to be at one of our events. Or, he could be supporting the next generation – our children/his grandchildren – in their endeavors with an encouraging word or cheering them at one of their activities.

Our dad was our hero. He was authentic. He was plain spoken. He was a man of action. He despised drama. He was every man and one-of-a-kind at the same time.

My youngest brother, Matt, appropriately labeled Dad "perfectly imperfect." The fact that he didn't claim or act like he had all the answers – and the fact that he didn't try to force his beliefs, morals, or lifestyle on us – made us admire him that much more. And it taught us two valuable life lessons.

First, you need to evaluate people based on the total package – the entire body of work – rather than on a one or two individual incidents or traits. That lesson was important for us personally – knowing that being perfect, while an admirable goal, was probably not achievable. It was reassuring to know that when we messed up, which we did regularly, all was not lost. We could still be good people and do good things.

It also was a valuable lesson for living with a spouse, raising kids, working with and/or managing people, finding and keeping friends, and in all other aspects of human interaction. It brings to mind the sage advice, "Don't let perfect become the enemy of good," and Peter Drucker's management advice to always hire outstanding people while understanding that people with great strengths have great weaknesses – "where there are peaks, there are valleys."

Second, it caused us to be more grounded, and to have a more balanced and healthy perspective about those we worked with and for over the years. While respectful, we were never star-struck by celebrities and others we met, or in awe of people we worked for. At times that created issues when the bosses expected more. But if we didn't put our dad on a pedestal, we reasoned, why would we put anyone else there?

Another of Dad's traits was, unlike some parents, he didn't view his status as "dad" to be automatic, a belief resulting from his strained relationship with his own father. Dad believed he had to earn the title and he was happy to do so. I don't remember him ever using any version of "because I'm your dad and I said so." He earned the designation by spending time with us, creating memories, treating us with respect, and letting our relationship mature as we got older. It was another good lesson for my brothers and me as we raised our own children.

I think my brothers and I would have been close to Dad regardless, but it probably would have been different had our mom not been in the car accident in 1966. I was fourteen and the oldest, and Matt, the youngest, was only five and in kindergarten. That "fender bender," as they called it, ruined my mom's life and forever changed life for the rest of us, especially Dad. The accident ultimately led to several dozen hospital stays and about a dozen major surgeries for Mom, along with the resulting battles with chronic pain, high-powered pain killers and their side effects, and the mental fatigue and turmoil from dealing with it. Over time, it destroyed my parents' relationship and led to their divorce in 1989 after thirty-eight years of marriage.

There were many days/months/years that Dad had to be a single working parent while also serving as Mom's health care provider. It was difficult and we watched and lived it, too. Dad got frustrated with the situation and sometimes wished Mom would respond differently. But he almost never complained and he never blamed Mom for the circumstances. He just got up every day and did what he needed to do the best he could. He tried to tune out the negative, stay positive, and make our environment as normal as possible. (Mom died June 1, 2005, at age 72.)

Fortunately for Dad, a couple of years after the divorce, he married Susan Willey April 19, 1991, and had nearly twenty-five years together. In total, Dad was married for nearly sixty-three years.

Dad's dream for us was the same as ours: that we would play sports professionally, preferably baseball. That dream faded for all of us, some sooner than others.

More realistically, Dad's goal was for the five of us to achieve more than he had, to be more educated than he was, and to be more tolerant than him. He also wanted us to avoid some of the errors he made and bad habits he developed, which my brothers and I had already swore would be the case. Mostly, Dad wanted us to grow up to be independent men who thought for ourselves, had the confidence to be ourselves, and had the courage to do the right thing personally and professionally.

For our careers, Dad wanted us to find something we loved and at which we could make a good living. He knew from his own experience that it could be a journey, so he was always there to support ours.

Dad kept things simple for us. His advice was mostly common sense stated in memorable ways, usually based on his own life experiences. Dad hoped that my brothers and I would emulate whatever good traits he had, add our own strengths and beliefs, and in the process become our own persons.

Don't get the wrong idea. This is not a story of kumbaya. We grew up in the 1960s, '70s, and '80s, so rebellion was the order of the day – long hair, Woodstock, civil rights, Vietnam War, rock and roll, assassinations, and more. We had disagreements about all of that, as well as curfews, which baseball teams to play on, and the relative merits of marrying young. Some of the discussions were animated and intense, but we never doubted the fact that Dad had our best interests in mind…no matter how misguided we thought his advice was at the time.

When he faced challenges throughout his life and career and marriage and raising five sons, Dad always fought back with his weapon of choice: humor. For Dad, it was a weapon with unlimited ammunition, and he used it with pinpoint accuracy and timing. Dad taught us what a great asset humor could be in life, from dealing with sorrow to maintaining humility. In our house, you learned to laugh at yourself out of self-defense. Humor was usually the common denominator for the memories Dad created for us.

This book is true and includes some of the stories I have told friends over the years. After they got done laughing, they invariably made the same comment: "I'd like to meet your dad sometime." Several did; I wish more had. It's too late now. Dad died from congestive heart failure on August 6, 2015, at age 84.

I am glad Dad had a chance to read the first four chapters of this book about ten months before he died. I tricked him. I told him I was working on a major writing project that was about eighty-five percent complete. I asked him if he would mind reading it and giving me his opinion. As always, he was flattered to be asked, but said he didn't know how much value he could add.

I gave the manuscript to him wrapped in plain white paper in an unmarked white box after a family dinner in Kansas City, just before I got in the car to head back to Springfield. He didn't realize the manuscript was about him until he got home and opened the box. Because by then he had to use a magnifying glass, he was up most of the night reading it.

He recognized some of content since I supplemented my own knowledge and research with information from two of his own writings: memories of his childhood written in 2003 and a summary of his career written in 2011. He helped fill in some blanks and updated the thank you list included at the end of this book. Most importantly, he got a chance to relive a lifetime of memories with a combination of tears and laughter. His reaction was almost worth the effort of writing the book.

I wrote this partially as a tribute to my dad – to capture the character he was and chronicle the impact he had on my brothers and me. I also wanted to convey the tremendous power he found in humor.

Dad didn't think anyone would be interested in reading a book about him. He might be right. But I believe his story will bring back fond memories for fathers and sons of that era, while inspiring parents, especially young fathers as well as their sons, the fathers-to-be. We'll see.

Here's to Dad – my last and lasting Father's Day tribute.

CHAPTER ONE

A name and advice to live by

Ever since he was capable of hating, my dad hated his first name: "Everett" – as in Everett Leon Kincaid, Jr. He liked "Leon" so he used "E. Leon" or sometimes even "Leon E." just to ensure people would call him "Leon," not Everett.

He didn't like being named after his father. Handing down the name through multiple generations has and does work well for many, including my father-in-law, one of my best friends growing up, and one of the college presidents for whom I worked. But it didn't suit Dad.

Not surprisingly, he never once considered continuing the tradition with my four brothers or me. I was always impressed that he and my mom, Darlene Ann Schrader Kincaid, came up with ten names that sounded like they fit together:

Paul Kent (born in 1952)

Lance Craig (born in 1954)

Eric Lane (born in 1956)

Kevin Brent (born in 1959 and died in 2009 at age forty-nine)

Matt Christopher (born in 1961)

Paul Kincaid

I was named for Dad's best friend, Paul Fink. They had become friends at Topeka High School where Paul's father had been one of Dad's teachers. Dad and Paul later were in the National Guard together, often getting into mischief. Paul attended and had a good career playing football at Washburn University in Topeka, went into teaching, and ended his career as principal of Topeka High.

"Paul Fink and I had many adventures together," Dad said. "He probably was the closest I ever had to a mentor. He was very supportive of me, helped me grow up, and scolded me when I did something stupid. I admired his character, self-confidence, and the genuine care he had for my well-being. That is why, with Darlene's agreement, I named my first son after him.

"It was a few years later that I told Paul that. Tears rolled down his cheeks as he gave me a big hug. I know I would have turned out to be a much worse person if Paul Fink had not been part of my life."

Five boys in nine years. When people gasped at the number and frequency, Dad's standard response was: "We had five sons, then we found out what caused it and stopped." That quip always got a laugh, so he never stopped using it.

A more accurate answer was that Mom had a miscarriage a year or so before I was born. I think Mom and Dad had it in their minds that the baby lost was female, so they tried to have a girl, but gave up after five tries.

Dad's relationship with his own father was never good. The most tumultuous event was when his parents, Everett Leon Kincaid, Sr., and Joye Glass Kincaid, were divorced in 1943. Divorce was not common in those days and it had a lasting impact on Dad, who was twelve at the time. He wandered the Oklahoma cotton fields aimlessly for two days after his aunt gave him the news. He blamed his dad for the divorce and resented his stepfather when his mother remarried. In retrospect, he realized both his parents shared the blame for the failed marriage, and he regretted how he treated his stepfather, Willis Jasper "Jap" Titus, in retaliation for the divorce.

"I am not very proud of that, or how I refused to truly accept Jap," Dad said. "He was far more supportive than my own dad had been, but I was still in agony about the divorce and I was willing to take out my wrath on him."

The entire experience caused Dad to delay his divorce from my mom until he was fifty-nine years old, even though they struggled with their relationship for more than a decade. By the time they called it quits, all five of us were grown and on our own, so Dad felt at least a little less guilty about doing to us what his parents had done to him early in his life.

There was another significant event that deeply affected Dad's relationship with his father and influenced how he raised my brothers and me.

When he was thirteen years old, Dad moved to Topeka, Kansas, with his mother and stepfather. A couple of years later, he spent the summer in Oklahoma City with his father and stepmother, Velma Stevens Kincaid, nicknamed "Steve." Dad made up some high school classes and played baseball on a team with friends from his childhood. The field where they practiced and played was ten miles from the house, and Dad walked there and back at least once daily.

Dad played well enough to make the city all-star team that summer and he was preparing to play in the all-star game. The details are still vivid for him all of these years later.

"I begged my dad to take off work early and come watch me play," Dad remembered. "He had not done that since grade school. He agreed and showed up about game time. I saw him and I was elated. I was energized."

Dad rose to the occasion, hitting two home runs, a triple and a double, and playing well at first base. His play was included in the *Oklahoma City Times* story the next morning, with the punch line: "He made an excellent effort to lead his team to victory."

"After the game, I bounded up to my dad and asked what he thought of how I played," Dad recalled. "He told me he had run into some guy he used to work with, visited with him all during the game, and did not see any of it.

"I was crushed, totally devastated. I wanted so much for him to be proud of me, so his lack of interest was really hurtful. That one experience was the basis for my effort to see every possible event in sports or academics or church that my sons participated in. I hardly got to all of them, but I always inquired about the details, etc., to be darn sure they knew I cared.

"That might be the only thing I ever did well, and it was, at least in part, because my dad treated me in ways that I vowed I would never do to my children."

Dad lived up to the promise he made that day, not only to my brothers and me, but to our children/his grandchildren, too. All five of us made the same commitment to our own children.

But the most important reason Dad did not like being a "junior" was not his relationship with his own father, but rather his intense desire to be an individual. He did not want the expectations or constraints, real or perceived, which might result. He wanted to be his own man. He wanted to write his own history. He wanted to be remembered for being "Leon," not "Everett Junior."

All of that led to one of Dad's favorite sayings for us as we grew up:

> ***Most things have been said and done already, so to stand out and be memorable, you have to find a different way of saying and doing things.***

That mantra drove him in his career as an advertising salesman, as a story-teller for my brothers and me, and even in his role as a grandfather. Interestingly, it is the same message being delivered today to potential entrepreneurs: to be successful, you must find a way to be different and to stand out.

Dad knew what Abraham Lincoln did when he used "Four score and seven years ago…" instead of "Eighty-seven years ago…"; and what John F. Kennedy did when he said "Ask not what your country can do for you…" instead of "Don't ask what your country can do for you…." Through their choice and order of the words, they found ways to turn the ordinary into memorable.

Dad taught us to find new phrases to use and new ways to express old ideas. New ways to present materials. New ways to connect pieces of information for a more comprehensive analysis. New ways to attract business and generate clients. New levels of service to customers/clients. New ways to host guests, both business and personal. New ways to make events/celebrations special. New ways to out-work the competition. New ways to surprise, appreciate, and honor family, friends, and colleagues.

Dad wanted us to find ways to be distinctive in our actions and how we expressed ourselves. He knew sometimes the goal would be to stand out in the crowd. Other times, it simply would be for our own amusement and satisfaction.

Standing out with new approaches was only one of the sayings we grew up hearing regularly. Some were original; others were adapted from the originators. Many became advice to live by.

Money is never an issue, as long as you have some of it.

That statement is simultaneously simple and profound. It applies to individuals, families, businesses, recreation and leisure, retirement, even death. Three events in Dad's life, one at the beginning and two later in life, illustrated this truth for him.

Dad's story is a familiar one from that era – his family was "extremely poor," but he didn't realize it as a child. He and his family were excited when they got indoor plumbing. He, his sister, and their friends were glad to have and play with discarded baseballs wrapped in black electrical tape and broken bats held together with nails. The family lived on potatoes, onions, and other vegetables from the garden – which were better anyway than the groceries they couldn't afford to buy – along with other inexpensive staples: fried eggs, pancakes, and oatmeal.

Uncles, aunts, and cousins lived in the same house with Dad and his family. More than one family member lost a job in the late 1930s and early 1940s. More than one had a car repossessed. None of this was unusual for Oklahomans coming out of The Great Depression.

Many of Dad's friends also struggled financially, so it seemed normal. Dad didn't truly realize how poor his family really was, not even when his grade school teacher asked the children in his class to bring money to assist a poor family living in the neighborhood.

Dad proudly presented a penny (worth sixteen cents in 2016) to the teacher to help the cause. Tears began to roll down the teacher's face as she accepted the penny and thanked Dad. It was much later that Dad learned that she was crying because the class was not raising money to help just any poor family in the neighborhood. It was for his family. The Kincaid family.

Fast forward about fifty-five years to the latter part of Dad's advertising sales career for farm publications. He had worked a number of years for what had become Harvest Publications. Then Harcourt Brace Jovanovich (HBJ) acquired Harvest Publications and converted the retirement of its sales force into shares of company stock. There was no discussion and there were no options – the employees had no say in the matter.

HBJ owned SeaWorld at the time, which helped make its stock strong. When it divested its theme park division, the HBJ stock value plummeted and the value of Dad's retirement (and the other sales staff) went with it – from thirty-some dollars per share to less than ten dollars per share. It was a bitter end to a long and successful career with the same company, and it caused Dad to question how committed large corporations were to the interests of their employees.

When Dad's time with HBJ ended, he signed on with Farm Progress. They moved him to the office in Des Moines where he lived and worked for two years. After two years in Des Moines, he continued with Farm Progress as an independent contractor, but moved back to Kansas City. Rather than asking for a salary, he signed an agreement with Farm Progress for a commission based on sales, with Dad covering all of his own expenses. The base commission was ten percent if his sales met the previous year's total, and twelve percent if he exceeded the previous year.

It was a good arrangement for Dad because he wanted to have control of his expenses, including his career-long practice of giving candy, popcorn, and other small gifts to clients. He also was convinced that he could get far more volume from the area if he was based in Kansas City instead of making the trip from Des Moines to Kansas City every month or two.

The mistake the Farm Progress brass made was to base the commission agreement on historical sales, not potential sales. In fact, they badly underestimated. With the twelve percent commission, Dad earned more than the president of the company in the first year of the agreement. So, they changed the maximum commission to ten percent. Dad made even more the second year.

Even as Dad was being named Farm Progress "Salesman of the Year," the company also changed the agreement in years three and four, finally getting him down to a "normal level."

"Then they 'retired' me," Dad recalled. "I was crushed.

"The final chapters of my career were okay, but not great. I went from selling ads in the number one publications in the agriculture category to representing publications that were marginal. They had good selling points, but were far from the number one buy in the minds of advertisers."

Dad continued to sell advertising in the Midwest for some agriculture magazines on a contract basis, but it was slow going and more than once he had trouble getting his commission check as publications faltered and ultimately failed.

For all of his advertising career, Dad fought to keep enough food on the table for five boys; deal with Mom's hospital stays and operations; pay the mortgage; and find a divorce late in life. Even so, Dad continued his childhood habit of generosity, often spending money he really couldn't afford to spend – from buying soft drinks for the team after baseball practices, to sending cards and gifts to family, friends, and clients for all occasions, and more.

As usual, Dad dealt with it through humor. "We didn't invent poverty," he would say, "but we sure did perfect it."

Finances were always a challenge, and I regret those challenges caused him to work longer than he should have had to, live differently in retirement than he deserved, and have very little to leave to his wife.

> *Try to avoid fights, but if you don't have any choice, remember: first, act anxious to get started, and second, there is no such thing as a "fair fight" unless there is a ring, gloves, and a referee.*

My four brothers and I were taught to respect authority and stay out of trouble. On the few occasions where we did have problems at school, for example, the discipline from the teachers and principal was the least of our worries. What we didn't look forward to was going home and trying to explain the problem to Dad. He was not impressed with any of our excuses.

On the other hand, Dad taught all of us to have self-respect and confidence – to defend ourselves, and to stand up for ourselves and each other when necessary. He spoke from experience.

Dad didn't talk about it until well after my brothers and I were grown, but our aunts and uncles let us know. In junior high and high school, Dad not only stood up for himself, but also was "the enforcer and protector" for his family and friends. Apparently, the phrase "…or you will have to deal with Leon…" was used more than once. And he lived up to the billing enough times to keep the reputation alive.

One of my earliest memories of Dad was when I was about eight years old and living in Topeka. Dad played on the Lowman Methodist Church softball team. He usually was the catcher, probably because no one else wanted to do it. In this particular game, team member Bob Smith's brother, Steve, was in town visiting. Steve was a former professional softball pitcher and coached a professional women's softball team. That night, he became a member of, and pitched for, the Lowman team. He was the ultimate "ringer." At a softball game. In a church league. The irony still makes me shake my head.

Dad and the batters both spent the night trying to catch up with The Ringer's variety of fast balls, risers, and sinkers. The best Dad could do was block the pitches somehow, which he did. He used the chest protector and mask more than his glove; I remember him being pretty sore for the next few days. The batters did worse than Dad trying to keep up with The Ringer's stuff and the Lowman team won easily.

After the game, one of the opposing players smelled a rat. He confronted The Ringer, who said he was guilty only of helping his brother. Therefore, The Ringer suggested, any anger should be directed at his brother, not him. So, the opposing players gathered and went to the parking lot to confront Bob Smith and other members of the Lowman team.

Like usual, Dad had stayed behind to pack up the two smelly dark green canvas bags with bats, gloves, balls, chest protector, mask, and other equipment. Now, he had one bag slung over each shoulder and was headed to the car. As he walked, he saw the group gathering in the parking lot and heard voices getting louder and angrier. Dad went on high alert and his pace picked up to a fast walk just short of a jog. Without breaking stride, he let both bags simultaneously slip off his shoulders to the ground. In a booming voice he asked, "Do you need some help, Bobby?"

The discussion broke up soon without any punches being thrown. But it was a good example of Dad's first lesson on fighting: if you didn't have any choice but to fight, then make it clear you were ready, willing, and able – even anxious – to get started. Dad's theory was that most people really didn't want to fight – they didn't want to get hurt, to be more precise – so if you were enthusiastic about the possibility, they would back down.

(I always wondered if Dad would advocate the same strategy in 2017 that he did back in the 1960s and 1970s. Back then, the most dangerous weapon anyone would carry was a knife, and that was rare, unlike today where deadly weapons are much more prevalent.)

Over the years, this first piece of advice worked more than once for my brothers and me. My late brother, Kevin, was especially adept at scaring anyone who messed with one of his brothers or him. Kevin was short and stocky with bright red hair. When he got a particular look and took the stance, no one really wanted to mess with him.

There were a few occasions for all of us, however, where our adversaries' fathers apparently had preached the same philosophy to their sons. That's when the second lesson on fighting was applied: there is no such thing as a fair fight except in boxing. Dad urged us to have the attitude that the opponent was trying to hurt us and we should protect ourselves, our friends, and our family. The object was to win and win quickly, no matter what it took. He was talking from experience.

When Dad was in the National Guard, he and some friends were headed back to the camp after a night out. They were in an ambulance that they had "borrowed" for transportation. A local resident stopped them on their way back to camp and told them a fellow guardsman had had too much to drink and was passed out on a bench nearby. Dad and his friends loaded the drunk into the ambulance and smuggled him past the sentries at the camp gate. As Dad's friends were trying to figure out where the guy's outfit was, the drunk woke up.

"He thought we were trying to hurt him and started swinging," Dad recalled. "We laughed at first, but he then popped my friend in the nose."

Without hesitating, Dad launched an uppercut. It was one well-placed, powerful blow, not like the choreographed multi-punch brawls that go on for several minutes in movies and on television. The guy hit the floor in a heap. Even so, perhaps because of his drunken state, he somehow staggered to his feet, allowing Dad and his friends to help him into bed.

The next morning, the military police surrounded the tent where Dad and his friends stayed. The MPs asked if the drunk was okay when they put him to bed the night before. Dad and his friends assured them that he was.

But apparently he wasn't. That one punch broke his jaw and his ear drum, and he had several teeth missing. Evidently, the extent of the damage was masked by the alcohol consumption.

Dad got dressed and took his master sergeant with him to the military police headquarters to tell what had happened. Dad was restricted to his tent until they sorted things out and confirmed he did not throw the first punch. Eventually, he was cleared and no charges were filed.

When my brothers and I had arguments with Dad, especially in our rebellious teenage years, I can assure you that this episode was always in the back of our mind. There was a line we were not willing to cross.

The "win-no-matter-what-it-takes" didn't always work out as it was supposed to.

In about 1976, Dad was wrestling at home with Kevin, who was a senior in high school. The intensity of the wrestling escalated. Neither Dad nor Kevin wanted to lose. I am quite sure at some point, Dad delivered a crotch shot. Kevin didn't take it well; he moved out of the house within days. While Dad and Kevin patched things up fairly soon and became close again, I know the incident bothered Dad for the next thirty-five years.

> ***There is a fine line between being "in the groove" and "in the rut."***

Dad had two things in mind when he used this phrase.

By necessity, much of Dad's life was routine and predictable – going to work when he was in town; going to the office to check mail and running errands Saturday morning; traveling to the same locations for sales calls; attending baseball practices and games. Because so much was routine, he consciously made himself try new things – eating at new restaurants, going to movies that he might not normally go see, visiting different towns, driving alternate routes to the same destinations. He never wanted to be a victim of complacency and he never wanted to get stale. He encouraged all of us to be adventuresome and not get stuck in a rut.

That was from his perspective. From the perspective of others, Dad did not want his being in a groove to cause someone else to slide into a rut.

Dad was consistent and dependable, and he prided himself on that, but he also did not like those traits to be taken for granted. If you did, you did so at your own peril – he despised it and he didn't hide it well. Dad was action-oriented and not afraid to do what needed to be done, no matter the task. Sometimes the results were not the quality someone else might have achieved – in cooking and cleaning, for example – but the tasks got done and they got done on time. He believed in and lived up to the Implementer's Creed: a good plan executed with enthusiasm and on time is infinitely better than a perfect plan implemented late or not at all.

In his personal life and in his work, Dad had no tolerance for being taken for granted, and he passed that trait on to my brothers and me.

Never get old – it's not all it's cracked up to be. (Or, it's not the model, it's the mileage.)

There is no doubt Dad did not think he would live as long as he did. He turned eighty-four in March 2015, and died August 6, 2015, outliving most of his friends, classmates, and business colleagues. Like most men and women of his age, he "cheated death" more than once. And, as a result, his view of death – and life – changed over the years.

When he was in his mid-forties, I think he was pessimistic about his longevity. He worried that with old age would come declining health that could drain the limited family resources. On more than one occasion, when he was in a particular mood, he would tell my brothers and me his wish.

"Son, when I can't function anymore, just take me out to the woods in the winter when it's freezing cold," he said. "Prop me up against a tree with a bottle of whiskey and leave me. The whiskey will be the anesthetic and the cold will let me go peacefully in my sleep. I don't want to be a burden to you and the family."

I knew it was serious since Dad didn't like camping or being in the woods; he didn't really like winter or the cold that much; and he rarely, if ever, drank any kind of alcohol, much less whiskey straight from a bottle. So, he got my attention by describing his death with three things he hated. I always chalked it up to his Cherokee Indian heritage, of which he was very proud, but mostly to his genuine concern of siphoning off more than his fair share of family resources.

Thirty years later, with aging and overcoming various health challenges, things had changed.

I recounted the "let-me-die-in-the-woods" story to Dad on his seventy-second birthday. He was noticeably taken aback. He denied he had ever said that. And he wanted to make it clear that if he had said it, he had changed his mind. No woods. No winter cold. No whiskey. No, no, and no.

He had triple bypass heart surgery in 1994 when he was sixty-three. There was not much time between the diagnosis and the procedure, which limited the amount of time he had to think about it. He only had time to check in, get prepped, and have the surgery.

Coming out of the surgery, he hugged his heart pillow, got the "this hurts like hell" look in his eyes, and survived. Eighteen years later, the surgery was judged to still be in perfect shape. The worst part of the procedure was that it triggered adult diabetes, which led to daily insulin shots and impaired eyesight, a terrible curse for someone who loved to read, play cards, drive, and go to restaurants where he needed to read menus. As usual, he accepted it, did the best he could, and never complained.

In 2009, my second youngest brother, Kevin, died of heart failure at age forty-nine. Kevin had fought a string of health issues from childhood, as well as weight problems and more than his fair share of demons. Regardless, forty-nine was too young, especially with a wife and two adolescent daughters.

It has been said that there is nothing worse than having to bury one of your children. It would be hard to argue that based on how Kevin's death affected Dad. In his mind, he had failed a son and, therefore, had failed as a dad. It caused him to think about what he could have done differently to help Kevin through his difficult times and to overcome his health issues. That second-guessing continued until Dad died a little after midnight on August 6, eerily just minutes after Kevin's birth date of August 5.

Kevin's death also caused Dad to think about how he would like his own funeral to be handled and he ultimately outlined his wishes in an email to his wife, Susan. It was forwarded to all of us. We knew it was official because it was one of the rare occasions when he signed it with his full legal name. It read:

> Susan:
>
> This is a list of my wishes for the handling of my death. It is prompted by the confusion and hesitation regarding the handling of Kevin's death.
>
> My wishes follow. If you find any less expensive ways to handle it, please do so. Saving your dollars is far more important than having anything fancy.
>
> 1. I wish to be cremated. Very cheap casket.
>
> 2. No cemetery plot. This way the family will not have to feel guilty about visiting the grave.
>
> 3. I would prefer that my ashes be taken to the old 3&2 fields on West 87th on a windy day, and emptied into the wind from the south park access on the west side of the baseball complex.

4. *Paul does eulogies well. It would be fun for him to give mine. Matt, Eric and Lance could contribute anecdotes, as well as ("sixth son" Bob) Brunker and (good friend Terry) Butzirus.*

5. *Ask whomever speaks to emphasize that my only prideful accomplishment was fathering five wonderful sons.*

6. *Tell everyone I died of AIDS, so they will not be hitting on you, Susan.*

7. *KNOW THAT I LOVE YOU AND APPRECIATE YOU VERY MUCH.*

8. *Ask all the boys to help you manage the finances. I regret not leaving you in good shape.*

Thank you for adhering generally to this scenario.

Love from Leon

Everett Leon Kincaid

Dad reminded us of this email when he had aortic valve replacement in 2012, in case we needed it. At age eighty-one, this surgery was more of an adventure than the bypass surgery had been eighteen years earlier.

First, Dad had to determine if he wanted to go through this operation at his age. He decided he wasn't ready to sit in the woods by the tree; he agreed to have the procedure.

Second, he had to decide between the pig valve replacement, which was typically good for ten to fifteen years, or the artificial valve, which usually worked for an average of twenty-five years. After he finished laughing, Dad assured the doctors that at age eighty-one, the ten to fifteen year version would probably get him to the finish line. Plus, it was less expensive.

Paul Kincaid

There was more time between the decision and the surgery on the valve replacement. More time to think. More time to worry. More time to think about the "what ifs."

In an attempt to minimize the worry – both his and ours – a couple of weeks before the surgery, he used an email to pose a number of questions. They included:

1. *After the operation, will my speech be in English or Pig Latin?*

2. *Will PETA demonstrate against me for animal cruelty?*

3. *After the operation, will eating pork constitute cannibalism?*

4. *Will my Jewish friends shun me because I am part pork?*

5. *Will I be allergic to pork chops and baby back ribs? How about bacon? Sausage?*

6. *Will "oink" be a large part of my vocabulary?*

It was one of those emails that made me laugh out loud. It certainly was more humorous than the email he sent to family members late the night before his surgery:

> *I do not think it really necessary to tell you how much I love you, how wonderful you have made my life. BUT – I feel it necessary to thank you for all the love, attention, and fun you have showered upon me.*
>
> *My thoughts will be of you as I head into this new adventure… and that will be why I'll be smiling.*
>
> *Much love,*
>
> *Leon, Dad, Brother*

That one was sobering and made tears well up, especially first thing in the morning. I read it on my iPhone when the first of my four alarms went off at 4:20 a.m.

Given that email note, I should not have been surprised about what I found when I visited Dad in the hospital two days after his surgery. He had most of the tubes out; his medications were being cut back, but the pain was still under control; and he was starting to get out of bed to sit in his chair and go to the restroom.

He was on the verge of euphoria. He had not planned to make it through surgery, to see all of us again, to still be alive. He was surprised. And pleased.

About a day later, however, the physical therapy began. Over the next few weeks, I am sure he wondered if he had wished for the right outcome. Recovering from that kind of surgery at any age would be difficult. Recovering at age eighty-one and not being in the best physical condition tested his willpower, his pain threshold, and even his sense of humor. Dying on the operating table under anesthetic would have been infinitely less painful.

The surgery worked and the recovery went well. I actually think it renewed Dad's determination to live whatever years he had left to their fullest, including spending as much time as possible with his family.

Once again, Dad had cheated death and, much to his delight, outlived even more of his contemporaries.

CHAPTER TWO

Driving in the DNA

You either grow up in a driving family or you don't. You can find a few exceptions, but not many.

Which kind of family you grow up in influences you for life. Later, it can be one of the most challenging kinds of "mixed marriages." I know from firsthand experience. When you disagree, who prevails? How do you raise the kids? Can a couple from such different driving backgrounds successfully coexist?

When you grow up in a non-driving family, even the shortest trips can trigger tremendous anxiety. First, you have to decide to make the trip. It is a huge first step. That's when all the fun begins.

Check the oil and tire pressure.

Let the dog out.

Shave, shower, put on makeup.

Get dressed.

Let the dog out…again.

Make sure all of the appliances are off and only minimal lights are left on.

Activate the alarm system.

Let the dog out...again.

Pack the cooler.

Pick which coat to take, just in case.

Grab a bottle of water for the trip.

Let the dog out one last time.

And, after all of that, at the very last minute, the non-driving family member is likely to announce that the four-block trip to the grocery store is just "too much" and not worth it. It can wait for another day.

It is an exhausting experience, to say the least, and it can make those from driving families go absolutely nuts.

Meanwhile, for driving families, all it takes is an invitation like: "Wanna ride along?" or "Let's go..." or even "Outta here?" You will be in the car and four blocks from the house before you even think to ask where you are going, how long you will be gone, and all of the other logical questions.

My brothers and I grew up in a driving family, at least on Dad's side of the family. Driving was and is part of our DNA. It was a combination of living in suburban Kansas City and getting to and from the various activities of five boys. It also came from the independence and freedom cars represented to the five of us – to most American males, for that matter.

Plus, there was an added benefit. When we were able to afford cars with air conditioning, there were some days (then and now) that the only place the warm-blooded Kincaid boys could get really cool on hot summer days was in the car. It was a small, enclosed space; you could recycle the air; and you could turn the temperature as cold as it would go.

Our love affair with cars was fed by Dad's career as a traveling salesman. He drove between 40,000-45,000 miles per year for about thirty-five years in a series of two-year leased cars provided by the company. It was and is a staggering number of miles, which I appreciated some at the time, but appreciate even more now. Three of my brothers and I ended up in jobs that require a significant amount of travel. An hour trip is a piece of cake. Any trip three hours or less qualifies as an easy "up-and-back." Five hours is plenty, but not hard.

Early years and family trips

Growing up in Johnson County and the township of Mission in the suburbs of Kansas City, there were two distances. It was "five to ten minutes" to the neighborhood park, the elementary school, the school bus stop, the high school, and many of our friends' houses. Every other trip was "twenty to thirty minutes one-way." That included downtown Kansas City, several shopping malls, the Country Club Plaza, and our baseball games and practices.

Since Dad traveled, many weeks Mom became the taxi driver for us. My parents wanted us to be active and to explore a variety of opportunities. All of us played multiple sports. Four of us took music lessons. I played in a rock-and-roll band briefly in junior high school. We were involved in church activities. We babysat and mowed yards to earn money. To accomplish all of this, it was necessary for us to spend a considerable amount of time in the car. And we did.

Most of our driving was in town or on short trips. We didn't take many family vacations. With sports and other activities, there weren't many windows of time all of us had free to travel. And, the money required for long trips was always in short supply.

The seven of us did make a few trips together: to Colorado to see the mountains; to Lake Texoma on the Oklahoma-Texas border to see Dad's father and stepmother; and to Mobile, Alabama, to see Dad's mother and stepfather. My mom's parents lived in Topeka, which was sixty miles away.

We went there more often, but it wasn't a long trip and, therefore, not as complicated.

We had a routine when we traveled long distances in Dad's four-door company sedan.

We planned ahead to save money. Our packing included a white squeaky Styrofoam cooler with sandwich ingredients (meat, cheese, mustard and Miracle Whip) along with a loaf of white bread, chips and other snacks, and Pepsi in glass bottles, which was the only way it came in the 1950s and 1960s. We ate in the car as much as we could. This saved money on food and also on hotel nights since we were able to travel further each day – we made each of the trips to Colorado, Oklahoma, and Mobile in a one day from Kansas City. The only real expense was gas, which was not insignificant even at eighteen to twenty-four cents per gallon supplying the thirsty gas-guzzlers of the 1960s and '70s.

For most of the trips, none of us were driving age yet, so Dad was behind the wheel virtually every minute of the trips. The one exception was the return trip from Mobile.

It was late December and Dad was exhausted even before we loaded the car to start the return trip to Kansas City. I had just started driving, and was able to drive with a parent in the car. So, Dad put me behind the wheel while he got some rest. Soon after I started driving, it began to snow. My lack of experience driving in bad weather, plus the pressure of having Dad and my brothers in the car – Mom had flown back because she couldn't physically handle the long car trip – caused me to hand the wheel back to Dad after only thirty minutes. A half-hour was not nearly the rest Dad needed, so we spent the last couple of hours doing everything we could think of to keep him awake until we pulled into the driveway. It was a struggle and we were probably lucky we made it home in one piece.

So how did we fit two adults and five squirmy boys into a four-door sedan?

To start with, we didn't worry about seat belts. In the 1960s, seat belts were the original stiff cavass-like lap version, which were only available in newer cars, and a long way from being required by law. So, our seating arrangement for "rest time" was as follows:

Dad and Mom were on the front bench seat in the driver and passenger seats, respectively.

One of us sat in between them in the front seat.

Two of us sat in the back seat, backs against the doors facing each other, with legs/feet side-by-side in the seat's middle space.

One of us, usually Matt since he was the youngest and smallest, got up in the back window sill. That was not much fun if the sun was out.

And whoever got the short straw had the floor board of the back seat. The good news about the floor board was you didn't have to share the floor space with anyone else. The bad news was that you had to figure out how to get comfortable with the "hump," the raised section in the middle of the back floorboard that accommodated the drive shaft of rear wheel drive. Spending any length of time on the floor board could put you in a bad mood, and usually did.

For most of the trips, we had "4/75" air-conditioning – that is, four windows rolled down driving at seventy-five miles per hour. Being warm-blooded, we celebrated when air-conditioning became a standard option on cars.

We played "license tag poker" to help pass the time. Back then, most of the license plates were comprised of five to seven numbers only, no letters. In some order, each would be assigned "the next car" from which you would put together your best five-number hand. For example, the Montana license plate of 29590 (pair of nines) lost to the Colorado plate of 2552 (two pair). Sometimes, we made it more interesting by declaring "deuces wild." With Dad and all five of us playing, we had to pass six cars to complete "a hand." I always thought the game was just a good excuse for Dad to pass cars and get on down the road.

Back then, there was virtually nothing we wouldn't eat in the car as we traveled. That included Kentucky Fried Chicken and pizza, both of which were fairly inexpensive meals for large families in the 1960s. I wouldn't even consider that today, and didn't when our kids were growing up. But back then, we wanted to eat cheap and keep moving.

The one thing we rarely did in the car was read. That usually led to motion sickness, which resulted in moaning and groaning and sometimes an urgent stop on the side of the road. That cost us time we didn't want to waste.

A parking lot

I got my first car in 1967 at age fifteen. Kansas law permitted you to drive anywhere with another legal driver in the car. It also allowed you to drive alone to and from school, and to complete a limited number of necessary errands for the family, such as driving to the grocery store. Having another driver in the family was helpful and soon-to-be essential after Mom's accident.

My uncle, Gordon Schrader, Mom's younger brother, helped me find my first car. In fact, he helped all five of us with cars over the years, more than once for some of us. He was city manager of Osawatomie, Kansas, and he and I had been close since the doctor slapped me on the butt at birth. Cars were less expensive in Osawatomie, which was important. My parents made a deal with my brothers and me: they would pay half the cost of our first cars if we came up with the other half.

The car I settled on was a red 1961 Chevrolet Bel Air with about 50,000 miles on it. My parents paid a hundred dollars and I paid the other hundred to cover the two hundred dollar sale price.

That was the first of many cars that would be parked in front of our house during our teen years. It was a smorgasbord of makes and models, but they all had a few things in common: age, high mileage, and questionable tires. It was the automobile version of rescuing a dog from the Humane

Society – take the ones discarded by others, overlook the flaws and call them your own, feed and care for them, and be loyal to the bitter end. Between 1967 and about 1981, alone or in some combination, the rescue vehicles you might have seen in front of our house included, in no particular order:

> Late 1950s Vintage Black Ford Fairlane 500 (shared with our mom)
>
> 1961 Roman Red Chevrolet Bel Air
>
> 1967 Champagne Oldsmobile Delta 88
>
> 1968 Oldsmobile Cutlass with Buckskin color body and Black vinyl top
>
> 1964 Guardsman Blue with Wimbledon White top Ford Galaxy
>
> 1966 Wimbledon White Mercury Monterey Breezeway
>
> 1970 White Ford Crown Victoria
>
> 1966 Buick Skylark Convertible Coupe with Shell Beige body and Riviera White vinyl top
>
> 1968 Two-tone – Moroccan Brown bottom and Tijuana Tan top – AMC Hornet
>
> 1969 Candy Apple Red Mustang Hatchback
>
> 1972 Ascot Blue with Antique White Landau top Camaro
>
> 1965 Ermine White Chevrolet Impala Station Wagon – complete with the police spotlight on the driver's side from its previous life (shared with our mom)
>
> 1979 Giallo ("Mustard") Fiat

1969 Covert Beige Oldsmobile Delta 88

1970s Vintage Dark Red Chrysler Cordoba

1964 Ember Red Chevy Impala

Believe me, the colors make them sound more glamorous than there were, but each actually did have one or more colorful stories associated with them. And if you are thinking that the collection outside our house must have looked like a second-rate used car lot, then you are thinking what a lot of our neighbors and friends said out loud.

We always left room in the driveway for Dad's company car since he was usually loading or unloading suitcases or baseball practice gear into it. For his part, Dad took the turnover in cars in stride, leaving it up to us to take care of them, fund repairs, and keep gas in them.

Apparently, necessity is the mother of invention

When Dad was fifteen and spent the summer in Oklahoma City, his father's house was on the north side of the city and the ballpark where his team practiced and played games was on the south side, ten miles away. Dad walked the ten miles to the Rotary Park field for practices and games, and then walked home again afterward. As you can imagine, that got old quickly.

Dad's father had a 1945 pickup that sat in the driveway. The tires were flat and it would not start. Dad suggested a deal to his father: if Dad was able to fix the pickup so it would run, he would be allowed to use it to go to practice and games. His father just laughed at him and said "sure." He never dreamed Dad could make the junk heap run. But he did.

Dad took each tire off one at a time, rolled it by hand six blocks to the nearest gas station, filled it with air, and patched the inner tube on the two tires that needed it.

He used his weekend poker winnings to buy a can of gas, which he carried from the station and poured into the tank. He carried the battery to the station and had it charged. He cleaned all of the spark plugs with sandpaper and cleaned out the distributor cap.

Finally, he washed the pickup with the garden house.

"I will never forget the stunned look on my stepmother's face as I started the pickup and headed to ball practice," Dad remembered with a smile.

What happened next speaks to the relationship between my dad and his father.

"Our practice ended about dusk," Dad recalled. "As I started to leave the park and head for home, my dad and stepmother showed up. My dad was mad as hell, even after I reminded him he had given me permission to drive the pickup if I could get it in running order. He said he was concerned about the bad brakes, no license tag, and no insurance.

"Since I got the pickup running, my dad was able to sell it and recoup some money, which he didn't think was possible before. By the way, he did not share any of the proceeds with me."

Fast forward fourteen years to 1960, when Dad was twenty-nine years old. Uncle Gordon was twenty years old and a senior at Baker University in Baldwin, Kansas. Mom and Dad offered Uncle Gordon the 1950 navy-blue two-door standard shift Plymouth that was parked in their back yard – provided, that is, Uncle Gordon could get it running. The car needed a battery, a muffler, and some other minor repairs.

Uncle Gordon did get it running and Mom and Dad made good on their promise – they gave him the car. Not only that, but Mom and Dad paid the taxes, tags, and insurance – with money they probably couldn't afford to spend. Dad had taken his own negative experience, spun it 180-degrees, added love and respect, and turned it into a positive one for someone else. And he never told anyone about it; it was fifty-five years later when Dad died that I first heard the story from Uncle Gordon.

In 2003 when I heard the story about Dad fixing the 1945 pickup, I should have been impressed and expressed admiration for his persistence and ingenuity. Instead, my first reaction was: "You've been holding out on us all these years!"

When my brothers and I were growing up, we only knew how to use two car tools: jumper cables and tow chains. That was twenty-five years before cell phones, so there was no immediate communication when you had a problem. Therefore, you might forget your billfold and you might forget your sunglasses and you might even forget your house key. But you never, ever forgot who had the jumper cables and chains with them, and you tried to know where they were at all times. Both the chains and cables got plenty of use over the years, especially in the winter.

None of us had a clue that Dad could fix anything having to do with a car; there were some days we thought he did well to know the key went in the ignition. It may have had something to do with the difference between the way cars were made in the 1940s compared to the 1960s and '70s. Just as likely, he let any mechanical talent remain a secret so as to manage expectations and keep control of his limited free time. Regardless, it was quite a revelation when we heard the story…and proved he knew how to keep a secret.

Road warrior

In the 1960s, the main worry most kids in the United States had was a nuclear attack. Russia was in the hands of communists and the Russian leaders made regular threats. The Cuban Missile Crisis had put everyone on edge. We had regular drills at school where we practiced crawling under our desks for protection from nuclear attack.

All of that was scary. But what kept me up at night was worrying about Dad as he drove the thousands and thousands of miles each year to sell advertising for farm magazines. He traveled early in the morning, he traveled late at night, he traveled when he was tired, and he often traveled on two-lane county highways and country roads, not divided four-lane highways.

I worried about us getting a late night call that Dad had been in a high-speed fiery accident and was in the hospital in Iowa, Missouri, Texas, or another state in his territory. I had nightmares about how I would react, what his body would look like after the wreck, and how our family would survive if he died.

The fact was, in all those business miles – 40,000-45,000 miles per year for about thirty-five years, or a total of more than 1.4 million miles – there were very few tickets and only two accidents.

The first accident occurred when Dad was on an unfamiliar narrow bridge and the driver in the oncoming car had the bright lights on. Dad was blinded, edged away from the glare, and glanced off the side of the bridge. The next few seconds consisted of the car careening back and forth between the two sides of the bridge as Dad, who rarely wore a seatbelt, was being thrown around the car, trying to find his way back to the steering wheel. He finally succeeded and got the car stopped.

Dad was okay, but the car was quite a sight. We knew about the accident, so Mom, my brothers, and I were waiting outside when Dad pulled into the driveway. Most of the outside sheet metal on both sides of the car was missing, dented, or scraped. All of us remember that the suitcase, which was in the back seat and was thrown around as the car banged across the bridge, looked brand new. It was quite an advertisement for the hard shell Samsonite.

In the second incident, a deer didn't quite make it across the road before Dad hit it. Dad was able to control the car and get it stopped. He pulled the dead deer off to the side of the road and continued home. The car was banged up, but drivable. What we all remember from that incident was how upset Mom was that Dad didn't bring the deer home for the meat. Never mind that we had never hunted, didn't own guns, hadn't ever eaten venison before, and did not particularly like the little bit of wild game we had tried. Money was tight enough that she just didn't want to waste fresh groceries.

What I came to understand was that Dad was a great highway driver. He knew how to drive in all kinds of traffic and in all kinds of weather. He always had options in mind if he got into trouble. And he always had the attitude that if the car was still on and he was behind the wheel, he could determine the outcome.

The five most valuable lessons I remember and taught my kids were: 1) always drive defensively and have an escape plan in mind at all times; 2) don't try to correct your mistakes too quickly – it will only compound the problem; 3) drive on the shoulder if you need to; 4) realize that sometimes it is safer to speed up, rather than slow down, to avoid trouble; and 5) when driving on ice, keep the tires turning to allow you to control the car, and avoid braking too hard which will lock the brakes.

He had other tricks, too, like snuggling in behind an 18-wheeler in fog or low visibility so the back of the rig outlined in lights provided a beacon to follow, or rubbing the tires along the snow piled next to the street for added friction to help slow the car if it was sliding, or watching the tires of cross-traffic vehicles to see if they were locked up, which meant the driver was likely not in control.

Dad's routine was about the same three of the four weeks every month. He would leave town on Sunday or Monday and return on Thursday or Friday evening. During the summer, he tried his best to plan his trips around baseball games. More than once, for example, he would be in town for a Saturday game and then leave early Sunday to make the twelve-hour trip to Houston so he could start his appointments first thing Monday morning.

When Lance, Eric, and I played college baseball at Phillips University in Enid, Oklahoma, he tried to schedule at least some of his Texas trips so he could catch a game or two. Sometimes he saw us on our spring trip in Texas or against Texas schools in our conference, but more often he timed his trip to or from Texas or Oklahoma so he could swing by and see us play in Enid.

Those were not the only side trips he made. When Hurricane Frederick went through Mobile and damaged his mother's trees and house in 1979, he offered to help. He went to Houston early for his business trip. Then he and his sister, my Aunt Jean, and her late husband, Uncle Richard, traded off driving the seven and a half hours from Houston to Mobile. For twenty-four hours, they visited, helped saw trees and branches, and cleaned up the yard, then made the return trip to Houston. Being from a driving family, it was no big deal.

And then there was in-town driving

Much later in life, I realized my fear for Dad's safety when he traveled was not based on his highway driving, but rather on his in-town driving that I experienced regularly. There was quite a difference.

If you were on the highway, there is absolutely no one better to be riding with than Dad. In town, however, you would be willing to pay money not to have to climb in the car with him.

Dad used the accelerator and brake with equal and alternating force – maximum acceleration, maximum braking. He followed and stopped close enough to the car in front of him that we could read the manufacturer's name on the tail light cover. And if he used his blinker, it usually was halfway through the turn, not in advance of it.

Growing up, our friends who rode with us got quite an education. More than once, sincere closed-eyed promises were made to the Almighty in the back seat, most of which, I am sure, were never fulfilled.

If you had eaten recently or were heading to have a meal, you were especially in trouble.

When I was driving age, I was among those who thought sixteen-year-old drivers were targeted by the police for special scrutiny every time they got behind the wheel. One time I was in the front seat riding with Dad when a policeman pulled him over.

"Sir, you ran a yellow light, you were speeding, and you turned into the wrong lane," the policeman summarize.

"You're right, officer," said Dad, "I apologize."

"Well, just be careful next time," the policeman said and walked back to his car.

No ticket. No warning. No lecture. That one was hard to stomach. Had it been me driving in the same situation, I know the results would have been different.

We were at a baseball game and parking was unorganized in a grassy field surrounded by a snow fence. We had arrived early for one of the first games of the day. When the game was over and we were ready to leave, we were parked in by other cars that arrived after us. Dad evaluated the situation and then slowly pressed the car's front bumper against the snow fence until it laid flat so we could drive out over it. Problem solved.

That was a good example of how Dad viewed cars: they were tools for transportation, not showpieces. He always treated them and used them that way.

When we got in the car for any kind of errand, there was one phrase we didn't want to hear: "While others squirm and squeal, we wheel and deal."

That was Dad's code for: "Boys, we have fifteen minutes to make a twenty-five minute trip, so hang on and try to keep your complaining to a minimum."

Whoever rode in the passenger front seat would inadvertently try to push a hole through the floor as if he had the ability to brake. Meanwhile, at some point from the back seat, someone would yell, "look out," to which Dad would calmly reply as he weaved through a series of near-misses, "let them look out."

I rarely saw Dad concerned about a close call, but there was one exception.

On a winter night before I was driving age, Dad was taking my friend Tom Smith home after a visit at our house. Tom and I were both in the back seat. Dad began to steer the car and line up for the tight ninety-degree right turn from Elledge Street on to Neosho Avenue where Tom's house was located.

About ten seconds later, we were perfectly lined up to make the turn, alright, but only after a 360-degree middle-of-the-road spin. It took our collective breath away and Dad quickly checked to make sure Tom and I were okay. Fortunately, it was late at night and no one else was silly enough to be out driving around on such slick roads. We have recalled that adventure many times since.

We always survived riding with Dad, but we also swore we wouldn't drive like that when we grew up, a promise we lived up to…more or less.

Dad taught us to drive with purpose – like we were being paid on commission, not by the hour. He encouraged us to take our turn and not to be overly courteous at four-way stops; to accelerate when merging; to use right turn on red when we could; to get into the middle turn lane and deceleration lanes like we meant it. To drive any other way was unpredictable and confusing to other drivers and, therefore, dangerous.

He wanted us to consider ourselves in control of the car as long as the motor was running. He even taught us to use the car as a weapon if we ever got into a desperate situation that called for it. These are lessons my brothers and I used and taught our kids as they learned how to drive.

Enough is enough

Dad was never boastful. He was, however, confident in his abilities, especially in his driving, and rightfully so. He also had a low threshold for whining and he despised drama of all kinds. All of that combined for a memorable example of Dad's personality.

It was a snowy, icy winter night in 1976. Matt was a sophomore in high school and still living at home. Matt and Dad, who was in his mid-forties, were watching the ten o'clock local news. The news anchor cut to a live shot of a reporter in downtown Kansas City where cars were having trouble getting up 12th Street from the Kemper Arena/livestock yards area. Some cars were spinning their wheels; others were sideways on the sides of the street. The reporter, dressed in winter gear from stocking cap to gloves, pointed and spoke in dramatic hyperbole, describing the "treacherous streets" and reporting that it was "virtually impossible" for vehicles to get up the 12th Street hill.

Dad became increasingly exasperated with the story, the reporter, and the live shot. He first started talking back to the television in a normal voice. Then he starting cussing at the tv in a louder voice.

"Those a--holes don't know how to drive," he said to the television set. "It's not that damn hard."

Finally, he had had enough. He said the magic words: "c'mon, son."

Dad and Matt got in the car and made the twenty-minute trip on I-35 to downtown Kansas City. They took the 12th Street exit and went up to the stop light, which was at the top of the hill that no one could get up.

Dad took a left on 12th Street. It is a four lane street separated by an eight-inch-high concrete median. He drove the 500 or so feet to the bottom of the hill where the median ended. As he reached the bottom of the hill, he slowed down only slightly, made an abrupt fishtail left turn around the median, and accelerated coming out of the turn so as not to lose momentum. Up the "impossible hill" they went.

The sound of the ice and snow cracking under the tires was drowned out by the thuds of Dad's hands on the steering wheel as he made hand-over-hand corrections for the skidding. Up the hill they went, weaving through the two lanes of 12th Street through the stalled, abandoned, and tire-spinning cars. All the while, Dad yelled insults through the closed windows at the other drivers for their incompetence and stupidity. He even took one hand off the wheel long enough to flip the middle finger "bird" to a couple of stranded drivers.

Paul Kincaid

Sitting in the passenger seat, Matt laughed uncontrollably. Later, he reminded me that Dad most likely did all of this on tires of questionable quality since we always had well-worn tires on our cars.

When they reach the top of 12th Street, they got back on I-35, drove home, parked the car, went inside, took off their coats, and sat down to watch the rest of the Johnny Carson Show.

Point made.

CHAPTER THREE

Seventeen jobs, one career

When he was a senior at Topeka High School, Dad and his classmates took an aptitude test to identify the profession at which they would be most likely to succeed. The test indicated Dad should go into sales.

"I was stunned and insulted," Dad recalled. "The idea of sales was the furthest thing from my mind. I wanted to go to Yale University and be hired by the FBI.

"Obviously, that did not happen."

As it turned out, more than once during his adult years he was mistaken for a member of law enforcement. It was an easy mistake to make. Dad was about five-foot-nine and weighed between 200-220 pounds, depending on his age. For most of his working life, he had a flat-top haircut and wore traditional wingtip tied shoes. He walked upright and briskly, always with a purpose. And, if the weather dictated that he wore a dark overcoat, he looked the part even more.

Ultimately, Dad did go into sales and had a very successful career selling advertising for farm magazines. But the road from high school to the sales career was a long and winding one.

Paul Kincaid

Seventeen jobs

For fifteen years from high school until age twenty-nine, my dad had seventeen different jobs. He was proud of the fact that he was never out of work more than twenty-four hours, but he did not really enjoy any of the jobs he had. That was the bad news. The good news, he said, was that those seventeen jobs provided a "basic education about people that would give me a strong basis for my sales profession."

His first job was at age fourteen when Ernest Dibble hired him to work in his grocery store on Huntoon Street in Topeka. He worked all summer there, learning the care and presentation of vegetables and fruits.

When Dad wanted to earn more money, Mr. Dibble let him be the checkout person on Sundays. There was not much risk – in the mid-1940s, very few people shopped on Sundays.

When Dad got restless, Mr. Dibble moved him to his drug store side to be a soda jerk. That did not last long because Mr. Dibble's son, Dan, played football for Boswell Junior High and Dad played halfback for Crane Junior High. Dad was fired the Monday after Crane beat Boswell by a big score, proving once again, Dad said, that "family comes first."

Working at Dibble's provided the experience he needed to be hired at the drug store at 12th and Kansas Avenue, just two blocks from where he lived.

He went from there to a warehouse job at the Kansas School Book Commission, which shipped books to schools throughout Kansas. That job ended on June 1 when schools closed for the summer, so Dad started working on summer construction jobs, earning one dollar per hour.

That fall, he started the tenth grade at Topeka High. He didn't like school, skipped classes, and finally got so far behind that he quit to again work construction so he could earn enough to buy a car.

"That came to an end one very cold day when I was in water up to my knees trying to shovel mud out of the ditch," recalled Dad. "I went back to school, finally graduated in 1949, and got a 1935 Plymouth for a graduation present, which had a seventy-five dollar 'mortgage' at the dealership."

Next, he got a job delivering the *Kansas City Star* in Topeka. In those days, there was a morning edition (*Times*) and an evening edition (*Star*) to deliver. The main challenge was having transportation to drive the routes – he constantly needed to repair his Plymouth and kept adding more routes just to cover the car expenses. The Plymouth was a two-door, had bucket seats, and was on borrowed time from the day he got it. At one point, the passenger side front seat collapsed and was unusable, so Dad just removed the seat and carpeted the space where it had been. Anyone who rode with him got in and walked to the back seat.

At his peak, Dad was delivering more than 1,000 papers twice a day. Dad hired kids to fold the papers as he "drove like a madman" throwing the papers out the window.

"This was my first adventure in capitalism," Dad said with a chuckle, "and it all fell apart when the car collapsed."

He next worked at Seymour Packing Company, which made dehydrated eggs. "The smell was terrible and the work not worth the meager pay, so I quit," he said.

His next job was as a bookkeeper at Central Bank in Topeka, which he did briefly while attending Washburn University in Topeka. He left when he and Mom decided to get married. He needed a different job with more income.

Dad worked on the production line at Goodyear. He hated it and quit when the 1951 flood shut the plant down shortly after they were married.

Next he worked for George Champney, "a crazy steeplejack" who did tuckpointing, building demolition, and other construction projects. It was a scary job under perfect circumstances, but apparently Mr. Champney constantly completed jobs in the most dangerous way possible.

"I quit after I got some of our family medical bills paid off," said Dad, "partly because George operated on short capital, and on Friday afternoons, it was like a car race as each employee drove to the bank. The last paycheck presented to the bank always bounced."

For a while, Dad worked as a switchman for the Santa Fe Railroad. In the 1940s and '50s, working for the railroad was viewed as secure, patriotic, even romantic. But one not-so-gentle reminder eliminated it from Dad's long-term career possibilities: he hated heights.

Heights trigger a fear in Dad like nothing else. He was fine as long as he was enclosed like on a plane or in a building. But out in the open, his stomach did cartwheels, even when he took the first step up a six-foot step ladder.

That all came back to him one wintery night when he was on top of an icy boxcar as it went over the Kansas River Bridge.

"It suddenly hit me where I was," he recalled, "and I didn't want to be there. I laid down on the top of the box car and hung on with both hands. There was no way I was letting go with one hand so I could wave the lantern like I was supposed to."

He quit soon after that.

Three times when he needed a job, Dad worked at Leed's Shoe Store in Topeka, a division of the Edison Shoe Corporation out of St. Louis. Harvey Crable, who served with Dad in the Kansas National Guard, was an assistant manager at Leed's and helped get Dad on when he needed work.

"I worked there at retail sales, but quit when I realized I was beginning to actually hate women." Dad recalled. "They were demanding. I had to develop patience. I would have cheerfully killed a lot of the ladies who came in, looked at twenty pairs of shoes, and then left when it quit raining without buying any of the shoes they tried on."

Franklin "Tud" Love was the store manager and cared about his employees, which was appreciated, given the long hours. Dad said Mr. Love inspired him to treat people with that same kind of respect and consideration.

The job at Leed's stood out because Dad had to fight to keep it. Literally.

One winter day a guy in his mid-thirties came in looking for a job. He had been the catcher for the Topeka Owls minor league baseball team that summer. Mr. Love thanked him for coming by, but told him there were no openings. The guy asked Mr. Love which worker had been hired most recently. Mr. Love pointed to Dad. The guy approached Dad and told him he was going to throw him out and take his job. Bad idea.

Dad was in excellent physical shape at that time and in no mood to put up with this uninvited visitor. Dad picked the baseball player up and threw him head-first into a large five-foot square cardboard box. Everyone started laughing, the guy slunk out, and Mr. Love apologized – said he had no idea what the guy was going to do.

Dad didn't enjoy retail sales, but he said it was instructional about human nature and how to deal with a variety of people.

Dad served in the National Guard for a decade, from 1949-59. It was a good experience and he had a great time, but he said he laughed every time he saw a billboard that read: "Sleep well tonight…your National Guard is awake."

"We were pretty much misfits when it came to being fighters for America," he said.

He hung out with Harvey Crable, Paul Fink, Eldon Brumbaugh, and Gene Echols, and they constantly found trouble to get into.

One time when they were stationed in Minnesota, they got bored and began racing inside, and then out of, a large brick building. The single doorway out was only wide enough to let one Jeep through, so it was a game of chicken, as well as a race. Dad was winning all the contests, ready for the championship race against Paul Fink.

Roaring into the lead, Dad got through the door first – just barely – but the rope that opened and closed the overhead door caught on the windshield of the Jeep and ripped it off. As the windshield crashed down on him, he realized Captain Kuhn had stopped by, was standing just outside, and had witnessed the race. For punishment, Dad had to drive that Jeep the 400 miles back to Topeka without the windshield.

"I almost developed a taste for bugs," Dad said sarcastically.

There were other National Guard antics, too, like fishing from a sixteen-person rubber lifeboat and stealing distributor caps from Jeeps with the driver asleep (literally) behind the wheel.

"The funny thing is, I was a private for the first three or four years I was in the Guard," Dad said, "but when I started getting in trouble, I started getting promoted. By the time I left the Guard to move to Kansas City, I was a staff sergeant."

He credits the friends he made in the Guard with helping him mature "from being a self-centered moody teenager to a more mature and fun-loving guy."

His first business-to-business job was selling classified ads for the *Topeka Daily Capital* and the evening *Topeka State Journal*. The classified ad sales director was George Bauer, a different and difficult boss, according to Dad. Due to diminished sales, Mr. Bauer had just fired his three-man staff and hired Dad and two other salesmen. Each morning at eight o'clock, Dad and the other two salesmen met at Mr. Bauer's desk, where he berated them for not selling more ads and said he would cheerfully fire all of them.

"The only problem with that was we kept doubling the sales volume each quarter," said Dad.

Dad did not instantly take to selling – he was hesitant to call on companies at first. He remembered walking around the block three or four times before getting the courage to call on a real estate broker who had a reputation for being mean to sales people. He finally did go up the stairs to the broker's office and eventually gained the broker's acceptance. Over time, the broker purchased a lot of ads from Dad.

One of Dad's clients was Dale Sharp, who had just purchased the Pontiac/Cadillac dealership in Topeka. It was 1955, about the time GM came out with V-8 engines. Mr. Sharp wrote very creative ad copy and bought space from Dad for nearly all of the ads to run in the *Topeka Capitol-Journal* classified section. The business boomed, which made Dad a hero to Mr. Sharp.

The friendship with Mr. Sharp, and those he made at the Oldsmobile dealership, came in handy.

After a year of fantastic classified ad sales for the *Topeka Capital-Journal*, Dad and the other two salesmen were "sick and tired of Mr. Bauer's threats," so they all quit the same day. (A few years later, Dad said Mr. Bauer died of a brain tumor, which helped explain why he had been so impossible.)

Dad explained his predicament to Mr. Sharp, who quickly hired him to sell used cars. The used car lot was at Fourth and Kansas Avenue.

Not only did he like working for Mr. Sharp and the sales manager, Gale Moorman, but Dad also was successful selling cars. The job, however, was seasonal and the pay was based solely on commission. I remember Dad summarizing it this way: "Son, in the summer we ate steak; in the winter, we ate beans."

When Mr. Sharp sold the dealership to Mr. Moorman, the new sales manager fired all the salesmen he didn't know. The new sales manager didn't know Dad, so he was gone, too.

Mr. Sharp heard about the firing and called to ask Dad to come back. Since he did not like the new sales manager anyway, Dad went to work for the Topeka Oldsmobile dealer instead.

When Dad sold classified ads for the *Topeka Capital-Journal*, he saw guys wearing suits in another wing of the office building. He asked what they did and was told they worked for a group of farm magazines – *Capper's Farmer, Kansas Farmer, Missouri Ruralist* – and *Capper's Weekly*.

Dad had become friends with Bill Ransom, who was a couple of years older and who had been both a teammate and competitor with Dad in amateur softball and baseball leagues. Mr. Ransom worked for *Kansas Farmer* and he found Dad a job doing sales promotion for the magazines. Dad wrote letters, planned ads, and even posed as a farmer in a photo for one of the ads. That job gave him a great foundation of knowledge about the magazines, their purpose, and their competitive strengths.

After about a year, there was an opening for a salesman and Dad got the job.

"That was the beginning of the career I loved," said Dad, "traveling and selling ads."

It was a career in agriculture advertising that lasted forty-six years. He worked for the Cappers Publications, which became Harvest Publishing and finally part of Harcourt Brace Jovanovich (HBJ) in Topeka from 1959-61 and then Kansas City 1961-91. He then worked for *Farm Progress* from 1991-93 in Des Moines, Iowa; then back in Kansas City as an independent contractor from 1991-99. Over various times in his career, his territory included Kansas, Missouri, Iowa, South Dakota, Nebraska, Oklahoma, and Texas.

The job that got away

Somewhere deep in Dad was the desire to be a race car driver, and it almost happened.

At the Kansas State Fair, he met a race car owner who had paid the entry fee for the stock car race that afternoon. His driver had fallen ill, so Dad volunteered to drive for him. The owner agreed, with the provision that he would use a registered race driver if he could find one before race time.

Unfortunately for Dad, the owner did find a registered driver in time.

"I was crushed," Dad admitted. "That is how close I came to being a world-famous NASCAR race driver. Oh, what could have been…"

Of course, those who rode with Dad would say that he did achieve that dream, just in a sedan on streets and highways rather than in a car with a number and advertisements on it going around an oval track.

Early lessons learned

During his advertising career, Dad learned eight lasting lessons for life, as well as work:

Lesson One: Honesty is the only option. No exceptions.

Dad's magazine wanted to promote a new Hay Expo farm show being held at Kansas State University in Manhattan. Dad sold seven or eight ads, but was disappointed that another five or six companies did not run ads with him. He was frustrated further when a competitor, the *Kansas City Star Farmer* newspaper, which also had an ad section about the show, carried ads from the companies that had declined to buy from Dad. To add insult, the sales representative for the competitor was a former coworker. On Dad's next round of sales calls after that show, each of the other companies who had run ads in *Star Farmer* asked where that salesman was.

"They were steamed because the salesman had lied to them about price, and had run the ads without final authorization," according to Dad. "*The Star* had to transfer him to Chicago; his name was mud. That lesson burned into me that honesty was the only route to take in sales."

That commitment to honesty was tested and confirmed a few years later.

A client in Tennessee made a chemical weed killer for soybeans. In preparation for the next meeting, the client asked Dad to check on test plots at the University of Missouri to see how the product was doing. Dad called his contact at the test plot and was told that that the product was "way too hot" to be of any use to farmers – it not only killed the weeds, it also killed the soybean plants, and might even have contaminated the soil.

Dad asked to record the phone call so he could play it for the client – he was not going to lie to sell a couple of ads. He was naturally nervous as he prepared to make his presentation to the client. At the meeting, he played the tape for those assembled. The reaction was unexpected: they all laughed, many of them so hard they had tears rolling down their faces.

The client had already discovered how badly the product performed. They had bet the advertising agency president that Dad would not lie about the results. It was a joke and a test all rolled into one. Dad's honesty cemented his relationship with them.

Lesson Two: Sometimes you don't get the credit you deserve.

Leading up to January 29, 1961, a conservative sales manager rejected Dad's suggestion to produce a special edition to celebrate the Kansas Centennial. The manager glanced at the sales plan, tossed it in a desk drawer, and said he would not mess with it.

When the publisher, Oscar Stauffer, called the manager a month later to ask what he had planned for the centennial, the manager assured him there was already a plan – and he scrounged around to find Dad's outline. The special edition was very successful, and the sales manager took full credit for both the advance planning and the results.

"I learned that some people have no shame about grabbing credit, while denying blame," Dad said.

Lesson Three: It is all about relationships.

As with any business, sales was all about relationships. Like most successful salesmen, Dad manually did forty years ago what Facebook and LinkedIn do today electronically. He kept track of birthdays; he knew the names, activities, and accomplishments of the spouses and children; he knew his clients' likes and dislikes of food and music; and he followed individuals as they moved from one agency/company to another.

A turning point in his approach to working with people had come when Mr. Sharp convinced Dad to take the Dale Carnegie course on self-improvement, salesmanship, corporate training, public speaking, and interpersonal skills. It helped him overcome his introversion, allowed him to develop his presentations skills, and caused him to see relationships from the other person's point of view. It was a life changing experience for him.

These are just some of the Carnegie wisdom – including in the book *How to Win Friends and Influence People* – that Dad took to heart and put into practice:

> "Inaction breeds doubt and fear. Action breeds confidence and courage. If you want to conquer fear, do not sit home and think about it. Go out and get busy."

> "Today is life – the only life you are sure of. Make the most of today. Get interested in something. Shake yourself awake. Develop a hobby. Let the winds of enthusiasm sweep through you. Live today with gusto."

> "Most of the important things in the world have been accomplished by people who have kept on trying when there seemed to be no hope at all."

> "You can make more friends in two months by becoming interested in other people than you can in two years by trying to get other people interested in you."

> "The royal road to a man's heart is to talk to him about the things he treasures most."

"When dealing with people, remember you are not dealing with creatures of logic, but creatures of emotion."

"Happiness doesn't depend on any external conditions, it is governed by our mental attitude."

"Speakers who talk about what life has taught them never fail to keep the attention of their listeners."

"Your purpose is to make your audience see what you saw, hear what you heard, feel what you felt. Relevant detail, couched in concrete, colorful language, is the best way to recreate the incident as it happened and to picture it for the audience."

"When fate hands you a lemon, make lemonade."

"There are four ways, and only four ways, in which we have contact with the world. We are evaluated and classified by these four contacts: what we do, how we look, what we say, and how we say it."

"If you want to be enthusiastic, act enthusiastic."

"Only the prepared speaker deserves to be confident."

"Most of us have far more courage than we ever dreamed we possessed."

"Flaming enthusiasm, backed up by horse sense and persistence, is the quality that most frequently makes for success."

"Feeling sorry for yourself, and your present condition, is not only a waste of energy but the worst habit you could possibly have."

Thanks to the Carnegie program, Dad learned he was a better salesman and enjoyed the work more if he found something to like about his clients.

"Many competitor salesmen were very contemptuous of the people they called on," he said. "I always made it a point to find something I could like about everyone I dealt with, which gave me an edge over the other salesmen in ag advertising."

Lesson Four: Maintain confidentiality.

Dad was in front of a St. Louis hotel talking with coworkers. He had just learned that Monsanto had approved its largest ad buy with his publication – worth more than $100,000. Dad was excited and started telling his colleagues about it as they walked down the street to their car.

Suddenly one of three men walking in front of Dad turned around and said to him, "I am a vice president at Monsanto. I am pleased that you are doing some business with us. Might I suggest you not discuss such information in public where the whole world will know about it?"

"Wow," remembered Dad. "I felt like two cents. It was a valuable lesson I never forgot."

Lesson Five: Words matter.

A person who had a great influence on Dad was Ken Constant, who was the vice president for advertising, headquartered in Chicago.

"Ken was a very educated man, a wonderful speaker, and I used him anytime I could get a group together to listen to our presentation," Dad recalled. "Ken was a student of words, always talked to me about my word selection. He told me, 'The right wording, the correct words, will bring people to your way of thinking, while some careless remark or poor English will distract the client, and you will not make the sale.' He was right."

Lesson Six: There is no substitute for being prepared.

Dad credits advertising agency executives Dick Dodderidge and Cliff Nothdurft with educating him about readership studies. Those studies became the foundation of his preparation and his sales pitch. Dad also anticipated the questions and issues his clients would raise, and had responses prepared for each. He constantly studied the products and kept informed about his clients, their markets, and their problems. His clients were eager to see him and, as a result, his sales increased.

Dad read vociferously to educate himself about his industry, as well as for pleasure. He was a fast reader and retained what he read. One of the frustrations for my brothers and me growing up was to give Dad a 350-page book for his birthday only to have him give you a detailed review of it at breakfast the next morning. He would start reading the book at 10:45 p.m. after Johnny Carson's monologue and finish it at two or three o'clock in the morning. Our quest became to find a book he couldn't complete in an evening, but I don't remember ever succeeding.

Lesson Seven: You can only succeed if you work with good people.

Dad credits his success to the assistants he had over the years: Rita Meiners, Janet Hanf, and Sandy Murray. They were protective of him, hard-working, accurate, and kept Dad informed of all the inside political stuff that he should know to protect himself, his job, and his clients.

Related, he built relationships with gatekeepers, who in most cases were the secretaries/assistants to the clients. He knew and remembered details about their lives, too, and brought small gifts when he came for appointments. Most importantly, he took every chance to make them look good to their bosses by giving them credit and complimenting their work publicly.

Lesson Eight: You cannot always judge a book by its cover or people by the way they dress.

At the Pennsylvania Farm Show, a bearded Amish farmer dressed in overalls and straw hat was buying a piece of equipment, a disc, which was priced at around $9,000, a significant amount in the 1960s. After he signed the sales paper, the farmer pulled out a huge wad of $100 bills from the bib of his overalls and paid cash. It impressed Dad and gave him another reason to always be respectful of farmers. And it reminded him not to judge people merely upon appearance.

Advertising as a contact sport

There is no doubt that Dad would have preferred to play professional sports for a living. He loved the competition, pushing past physical barriers, and he even embraced the pain that came along the way. Since that didn't work out, he took that competitive spirit and applied it to his work.

Early in his sales career, he realized that all the agriculture ad sales representatives stayed at the same hotel, drank together at the hotel bar each evening, and traded information about clients they all called on. Salesmen would report what they had experienced or heard and, based on that, some of the other salesmen would decide they would not bother calling on those advertisers.

"I realized this was a loser's way of covering the territory, so I never developed the habit of being friendly with competitors," Dad said.

Some years later, his company's California representative was making a pitch to the Shell Chemical Company and its agency. Dad was with him at the presentation. The California representative told the Shell executives he had a large family and needed their business to help his income. One of the Shell executives, responded: "But the other (competitor) rep has a family, too." Without missing a beat, the California rep said, "Screw him and his damn family! Now get me those ads!"

"That was my attitude during my career," Dad said.

There was competition internally, too.

Although Mr. Ransom had hired Dad, apparently he was jealous of Dad's success and tried to undermine him. The two shared a secretary who told Dad in private that Mr. Ransom had been going through Dad's mail while he was on a business trip, pulling out space orders, and submitting them as his own in order to get the commission.

Dad was furious and confronted Mr. Ransom about it. Actually, it sounds like Dad did most of the talking while Mr. Ransom listened, backed up against the wall, suspended several inches off the floor by the front of his shirt, courtesy of Dad.

And then there was the race.

Dad got teased regularly about his weight and people assumed from his stocky, thick physique that he lacked athletic ability. That was a mistake. One day at his Cloverleaf Office Building at Metcalf and Highway 56 in Mission, Dad had had enough. He challenged his younger, seemingly fitter tormenter to a race – right then in the parking lot. So, dressed in his suit pants, shirt and tie, and barefoot, Dad proceeded to not only win the race, but win it decisively. And the teasing stopped…at least for a while.

Designated driver

Early in his career, Dad met and worked with owners, sales managers, and advertising agency representatives. They taught him a lot. He spent lots of evenings just listening to them talk about their business, what problems they had, and brainstorming solutions.

A lot of those talks occurred in Dad's hotel room. Kansas was a dry state back then, so Dad had a briefcase specially designed to hold three bottles: bourbon, scotch, and vodka. He was able to buy mixes for these drinks, and he got the reputation for being "the guy who could pour a good drink (free) anytime."

It didn't take Dad long to learn that alcohol was the center of all entertainment for many salesmen. Originally, he mistakenly thought his clients wanted him to drink with them.

"Thankfully, I realized early-on that this was not true," he said. "I did not like the taste of liquor, so I soon got off that kick and was much happier all my life without that burden."

If he needed reinforcement for that decision, he got it frequently. Several of his coworkers in Kansas City and across the country were alcoholics, as were some of his clients. Over the years, he carried and drove intoxicated coworkers back to their hotels, put them to bed, and kept them away from clients to avoid disaster. He watched them pad their expense accounts to fund their drinking habit. He even fished one drunk colleague out of the hotel swimming pool when he fell in with his business suit on.

There were dozens of other episodes, but there was one particular one Dad told my brothers and me. He wanted to make the point. And he did.

A sales rep from the New York office was an alcoholic. One morning, another of Dad's coworkers took him aside to watch. The New York rep was at the hotel bar to get a drink before breakfast. The bartender placed the drink in front of him. The bartender then got a large white tea towel, put one corner of it in the rep's left fist, wrapped it around the rep's neck, put the other corner in the rep's right hand, and placed the drink against the towel. The rep gripped the towel and drink with his right hand, then, with his left hand, pulled the drink up to his mouth using the towel as a pulley. It was the only way he could get the glass to his mouth without spilling it. That first drink steadied him enough so he could function.

"I decided alcohol was not going to be a part of my future," Dad said, "and I didn't want it to be part of my sons' lives either."

Standing out in the crowd

Being unique and memorable – standing out in a crowd – was important to Dad.

From Mr. Constant, he learned the habit of giving small, inexpensive, but meaningful, gifts to clients. (He did the same thing for family – when he came to visit us, he usually brought chocolates for my wife and a tin of popcorn for the kids; later, when my son began to play golf, he would bring a sleeve of balls.) He was reimbursed for some of the gifts to clients, but bought many on his own – an investment in future sales.

He sent hundreds of cards every year for all occasions: birthdays, anniversaries, thank you's, holidays. The cards were divided into two categories: traditional and "adults-only." Over the years, a number of people on the traditional list asked to be moved to the adults list. There were special situations where Dad would send multiple cards within a day or two – sometimes as many as two dozen.

He found different and interesting ways to make presentations. In the fall of 1964, he arranged a presentation over lunch. There were sandwiches and soft drinks, and there was a television so everyone could watch the World Series game between the Cardinals and Yankees. (The games were all played in daytime in the 1960s.) During the commercials each half-inning, Dad did a portion of his flip-chart presentation. It was entertaining and successful.

It was not unusual for him to take his clients to a nearby public park and make a presentation over a picnic lunch of fried chicken, or to have a barbecue lunch brought in, complete with red-and-white checkered table cloth and napkins.

Not all of the ideas worked out so well.

One Halloween he had a business dinner at the home of a client and his wife. Dad thought he would get into character for the holiday so he bought a big, scary mask to wear. When he got to the house, he put the mask on, grabbed the candy, popcorn, and briefcase, and headed toward the front door. The mask did not fit well and Dad could not see clearly out of it, which caused him to run into a four-foot-tall cactus. He got out of the cactus, continued to the door and rang the doorbell. His host and hostess both let out screams when they opened the door. Dad was wearing a white dress shirt, which now had his blood all over it. It took two hours to pull all of the thorns and get Dad patched up.

Dad also found memorable phrases and descriptions to use. Following a pitch to a Houston agency, he was asked why the client should remain with Dad's publications rather than go with the competitor. Dad was prepared. He dramatically pulled out a large single card mounted on a base. It read, "Covering the farm market with Big Farmer is like trying to fertilize forty acres with a fart!" The group laughed, Dad got the ads, and the agency president kept the card as a souvenir.

But Dad was best known for the Christmas lunches he held separately for about five ad agencies in Kansas City and Iowa. They became legendary. The agencies argued about which eight to twelve people got to attend. Dad gave each of the account executives raunchy gifts and even raunchier personalized limericks. One by one, Dad would hand out the limericks to the account executives who would read them out loud before passing them around for all to read a second time. It grew to where Dad was creating dozens of individual limericks every year for clients and friends, totaling some 300 for the years he wrote them. Even now, it's not unusual to have former colleagues, friends, and family members recall specific lines from those limericks.

Here is one of the cleaner, less suggestive examples:

THE SHOPPER

Miss Kristi, Queen of all Ebay
Had a thought on Thanksgiving Day
She thought it'd be a ball
To shop early at the mall
Finish her Christmas shopping that way.

Remember it had been years or more
Since Kristi had been in a retail store.
She was an Internet buyer
Knew retail stores were higher
Did not realize her decision was poor.

The first thing I saw was a helluva crowd

Paul Kincaid

All yelling, shoving, and being very loud
I finally got in the door
Already completely sore
But the low prices really had me wowed!

I first went to the Dayton store
Struggled to get into their front door
My skirt came un-zipped
I immediately tripped
And ended up on the Empire Mall floor!

A woman rushed over, grabbed my skirt
Didn't even ask if I was hurt
That selfish jerk
Just paid the clerk
I was left with undies, shoes, and shirt!

I was then getting very pissed
Started using my elbows and fist
I bought Doug some sox
Couldn't get a gift box
That was the only buy on my list!

The other shoppers did not even care
That I was embarrassingly near bare
As I left I had a wreck
Messed up my pretty Aztec
At times life just isn't fair!

Now I will always sit in my den
Do my shopping on Ebay again
I don't want shopper strife
To mess up my personal life
Doug, we'll even have more time to sin!

And the lecture was over

When Harvest Publishing and our family moved to Kansas City, Dad took over the Skelly Oil account. Skelly had nice quarters in the Country Club Plaza and advertised both their petroleum and liquefied petroleum gas appliances with the Harvest publications. Following the sales call, Dad invited the vice president and his two assistants to be his guests at lunch.

"They were flabbergasted," Dad recalled. "The previous salesman had called on them for years, sometimes talked up to and into the lunch hour, and never offered to treat them for anything. I benefited by being compared to him and I sold them a lot of ads over the next couple of years.

"I learned another lesson I never forgot: fiscal responsibility can very easily be overdone and can hurt sales efforts."

There was no doubt Dad spent more money on entertaining than any other ad salesperson. Not even close. And, I know he didn't submit all of it for reimbursement; he covered some personally. I can remember my parents discussing how to manage the paperwork and reimbursement checks in order to pay the American Express bills on time. Some months, it created a significant amount of stress.

While he had high expenses, Dad routinely outsold his colleagues, sometimes doubling or tripling their sales. That was both a matter of competitive pride and increased income since there were commissions and year-end bonuses at stake.

What frustrated Dad was how the accountants ignored the relationship – strong relationship, in Dad's opinion – between the entertainment expenses and sales. He always wanted the accountants to see the bigger picture and think about a "net" of the two. Dad believed in the adage that you have to "spend money to make money."

The concern over Dad's expenses led to "The Lecture."

Paul Kincaid

Every year, the company would have an annual sales meeting for its twenty-person sales force from across the country, along with their spouses. The week-long trip mixed business and pleasure in places like St. Thomas, Virgin Islands, Florida resorts, Las Vegas, and on cruise ships. For several years, it was one of the highlights of the year for my parents who made it double as a vacation away from the five of us.

During the business part of one sales meeting in the mid-1970s, the topic was expenses. It was one of those times when the talk was to the entire group, but the target was one person. In this case, that person was Dad.

The accountants talked about how expenses had been increasing and the need to keep them under control. Then the lead accountant started his lecture, giving the goal and some illustrations.

"We want you to have on the road what you have at home. That is what we are willing to pay for. Nothing more, nothing less. For example…

"All of you live in nice houses, but you don't live in mansions or even in the most expensive homes in your neighborhoods. So, on the road, don't stay at the Ritz Carlton. Stay at a Marriott or Best Western or Holiday Inn. We want you to have on the road what you have at home. That is what we are willing to pay for. Nothing more, nothing less.

"And you all have decent cars, but you don't have high-priced luxury cars. So when you rent cars on the road, don't rent a Cadillac, rent a Chevrolet or Ford. We want you to have on the road what you have at home. That is what we are willing to pay for. Nothing more, nothing less.

"And you occasionally have nice dinners at home, but you don't have steak every night. So when you are on the road, have a steak once in a while, but have chicken or hamburgers or something else most nights like you would at home. We want you to have on the road what you have at home. That is what we are willing to pay for. Nothing more, nothing less."

At this point, Dad raised his hand.

"Yes, Leon, a question?" the accountant asked.

With a straight face, Dad said: "At home, I have sex about twice a week."

The other salesmen couldn't control their laughter.

And the lecture was over.

CHAPTER FOUR

Embarrassing inspiration

It happened fifty years ago and my dad and I never talked about it again. Not once.

I didn't tell my mom before she died. I didn't tell my brothers, my wife, my children. No one. I doubt Dad did either.

Sometimes when I flash back to that moment, I physically shiver, trying – unsuccessfully – to discard the memory like a polar bear discards water after climbing out of the Arctic Ocean. Other times, I recall it as one of the most inspiring events in my life.

I was nine years old and I was mad at my dad. I don't even remember what I was mad about, but I was mad. I think every male goes through the "angry young man" phase. For some of us, it starts earlier and ends later. Or, perhaps it never ends.

Dad asked me to sit in the chair with him and tell him why I was so upset. That led to the embarrassing – and simultaneously inspirational – moment.

There is no logical explanation for what happened in those few moments in 1962. There is no excuse. It was a single event that defies explanation even after all of these years. Before finishing this story, perhaps recounting other memories will help explain why that particular event remains such an aberration.

Bedtime stories

Dad told great bedtime stories and he told them frequently. The stories usually featured either Sergeant Rock or Admiral Rock, depending on if it was a story about the Army on land or the Navy at sea. Anyway, the good guys always got themselves into life-or-death situations and had to out-think and out-fight their enemy to escape or win the battle.

The stories were not gory or vicious; they were thoughtful and creative. They were stories of courage and ingenuity. They were about good guys who became heroes. The stories always included lots of details as Dad painted a picture with the color of the clothes, the size of the guns, the glint in their eyes, and more. He made the stories up as he went and each one was different.

When he returned from a week-long business trip, one of our first requests of him was to tell us a bedtime story. I am sure that there were weeks when he would have preferred to collapse from exhaustion or watch television or do anything else after a long week of traveling, but I don't remember him ever telling us "no."

In addition to the stories, he would tell us about something he had done on the trip – going to a ballgame, spending time at a museum or zoo, eating at an unusual restaurant, or meeting an interesting person. He provided the same details and excitement in those stories that he did the combat stories.

I think he enjoyed telling us the stories, but not nearly as much as we enjoyed hearing them. They are among our fondest memories.

Christmas traditions

With five boys full of anticipation, Christmas was a special time. I am quite sure my parents stretched further than they should to make it so.

With the five of us, there usually wasn't a lot of sleep Christmas Eve. The split-level house we lived in had a lower level room where we all slept. We got to the room by going down some stairs from the living area to the garage, which we had turned into a billiards/storage/play room. A few more stairs took us to the lower level room.

To ensure there was no peeking, my parents would lock the door from the house to the garage. When any of us tell this story to our friends, it sounds mean; at least that's the reaction we get. We saw it as both necessary and funny.

Each of us had our "chair" for Santa's presents. We each got a piece of clothing – a pair of jeans, a shirt, or a coat – and one fun item, plus a stocking filled with candy, fruit, and nuts. There was always one game for all of us to share and play, which we did endlessly on Christmas Day and in the days that followed.

But the memory my brothers and I most remember is the Christmas Eve family dinner and movie. Usually in the cold and snow, we dressed up, squeezed in the car, and headed to one of Kansas City's steak houses or the Gold Buffet. It was special for us to be going to a nice place to eat and to be dressing up to do so. And then it was off to a premier movie at a packed theater. It was especially fun if it was a Sean Connery James Bond movie. What more could five growing boys ask for? Action, good music, and the Bond girls.

Games, games, and more games

We were raised to be competitive – with Dad, with one another, and especially with others. That was the case with every game we played, and there were lots of them.

One of the first games Dad taught us was dice baseball. We used lineups of real Major League Baseball teams and rolled a pair of dice to determine every aspect of the game. There was a different number legend for at-bats (balls, strikes, fouls, hits); the type of hit (ground ball, fly ball, line drive); outcome for each type of hit (out, single, double, triple, home run); and separate guides for specialty situations (steals, double plays, sacrifice bunts, sacrifice flies). I don't remember all of the details, but I do remember rolling a two, seven, or twelve always led to the best results.

Once you knew the rules, it would take about thirty to forty-five minutes to play a nine-inning game. We not only kept score, we kept cumulative player stats, team stats for the season, and, of course, wins and losses. Among Dad and the five of us, we played thousands of dice baseball games over the years. It was cheap, you could use your imagination, and it was competitive.

For Christmas one year, the five of us got a vibrating ice hockey game. Another year, it was a carom game. These games were great hits. Most board games didn't have enough action or involvement to keep our attention.

Another game Dad invented, or at least perfected, was Bombardier. Using scrap wood pieces from the lumber yard, metal play trucks and tractors, and whatever else we could find, we made forts facing each other about six feet apart. Usually the forts would stretch for four to five feet in width and be about twelve to eighteen inches deep.

Each side would get the same number of two and a fourth inch tall hard rubber soldiers/cowboys/Indians to place in the fort – usually around fifty to one hundred each…as many as we could round up and divide evenly. The rubber men had to be at least partially visible and could not be wedged in; they had to be able to fall down completely to the floor. It would take thirty minutes or more to set up for one game.

Then, using three to five golf balls, each side would take turns trying to "blow up" the fort and "kill" the men by knocking them completely down; pieces that were only partially down were still "alive." When tossing the golf balls, you had to lob them underhanded, thus the Bombardier name. The first one to knock down all the opposing men won.

We played Bombardier for hours in our double garage that had been remodeled into a game room. Again, it had the "Three C's" we always sought in games: cheap, creative, and competitive.

At some point, we graduated to another game that all of us took seriously: snooker. One Christmas in the mid-1960s, Dad wanted to use the $200 Christmas present from his father and stepmother to buy a pool table, but he couldn't find one that cheap. So, staying with the billiards theme, Dad found and bought something he could afford – a used snooker table, which he had assembled in the garage, which had yet to be turned into a game room.

Many hours were spent trying to be the house champion. It was especially frustrating for those of us who were away at college and came back for weekends and holidays. We didn't know how to use the "home field advantages": the garage floor sloped slightly, so you had to play the tilt; and there were metal floor-to-ceiling structural supports in the garage which forced you to be a contortionist and use a special short cue to make certain shots. As you might imagine, there was glee, not sympathy, when any of us got frustrated and complained about the playing conditions being unfair.

Later, Dad helped us all learn how to play many different versions of poker. He organized a monthly poker group that played together for more than a quarter-century. Over the years, my four brothers and I sat in occasionally – Kevin and Matt more than the rest of us.

Dad loved games and shared that love with all of us.

Baseball

We grew up loving sports of all kinds and over the years the five of us played many sports at varying levels of skill: football, track, racquetball, tennis, table tennis, pool, snooker, basketball, and golf. But Dad's first love was baseball, and it became ours, too.

Dad started pitching batting practice to us when I was around eight or nine years old. He knew that repetition and confidence were the keys to hitting well. He continued pitching batting practice into his forties. You could fill a good sized stadium with the players that benefited from his batting practice pitching.

Looking back, and having thrown batting practice myself, I can say that he was, truly, an iron man when it came to pitching batting practice. Dad coached or managed baseball teams for the five of us for a total of about seventeen years. At practices twice per week, he would give the fifteen or so players about ten to fifteen hits each. Accounting for misses and pitches out of the strike zone, he threw around 400 pitches per week during baseball seasons for about ten years. He threw without a catcher, so he had no real target. And we were not smart enough to have a grocery cart or waist-high basket stand to hold the balls, so he had to bend over constantly to fill his catcher's mitt with balls, which significantly increased the physical strain.

He also played pepper with us on our front lawn. For many hours over many years, he stood in the driveway with the cars as the backstop, hitting grounders and soft line-drives that we fielded and threw back for the next. Our split level house was on a hill, so the yard sloped down sharply to the driveway. That meant that when Dad stood on the driveway, his waist and swing were about level with the grass. Whatever skill we had as fielders was largely due to those hours of playing pepper on the front lawn.

Overall, having Dad as the manager was a good experience. We do still laugh about the time Matt got mad and quit the team. Apparently Dad didn't think Matt was trying hard enough or producing as well as he should. Matt begged to differ. There was quite a bit of tension around the house for a week or so until Matt decided to rejoin the team. Fortunately, Matt and Dad got things squared away pretty quickly with no long-lasting effects.

All of us remember a couple of things about Dad managing, both of which were a result of his own experiences. First, he always admired, praised, and found some playing time for those who had less natural ability, but who showed up for every practice, tried their best, and never complained. Second, he always had a soft spot for players who did not have a father, either through death or divorce. He empathized with them, talked to them more often, and had even more patience than usual. It was yet another way he gave back.

To his credit, Dad knew when to hand off the managerial duties to others. At that point, he became an interested and enthusiastic fan and supporter, a role he continued to play through our college playing days.

The Dating game

Dad was always a lot more confident in our ability to date than we were. Honestly, it just didn't happen very often for me; a couple of my brothers had more success. All five of us got married and had kids, but you might have to chalk that up to luck more than talent.

All of us had late night talks with Dad. He would be up when we got home, no matter how late, usually in a quiet house reading a book. He would greet us, put the book down, ask how the night went, and just listen. We had the same affliction as many of our fellow male teens: the fear of rejection, which made us hesitant to ask girls out on dates. He was empathetic and supportive, never judgmental. He always encouraged us to be more confident, to ask for dates, to not be discouraged if the answer was "no" or if every date wasn't a success. His support helped get us through the trying teenage years.

One of the nicest things Dad ever did for my brothers and me was to take us on "dry runs" of driving routes for dates. Remember, this was around the time GPS was invented in the mid-1970s, but long before it was first available in cars in about 1990. The dry runs were back in the day where you had a collection of large paper maps in the car, none of which you could correctly refold.

If we were going downtown, or to a new location, or moving between unfamiliar locations, he would offer to go with us as we drove the route a day or two before the date. The way he did it was helpful, not degrading. He never pushed or insisted; the conversation just naturally led to the dry run. It did provide a comfort level that we would not have had otherwise. I am not sure how many dads would do that, but I would imagine it isn't many.

Of course, another way to look at it is that he thought we needed all the help we could get. He was right about that.

Those dry runs also were handy for new ballparks, new work locations, and other occasions where you wanted to be on time, make a good first impression, and/or stay out of difficult neighborhoods. My brothers and I have continued that with our kids.

Education expectations

Dad told anyone who would listen that one of his proudest achievements was having all five of his sons graduate from college. Lance and Eric each graduated in four years from Phillips University; Kevin, going part-time while working, took longer, but graduated from Mid-America Nazarene in Olathe, Kansas; and Matt graduated in three and a half years from Emporia State University in Emporia, Kansas, where I happened to be working at the time.

Meanwhile, I was on the "three school, five year plan," attending College of Emporia one year, Kansas State University two years, and then graduating from Phillips after two more years. I played baseball at Phillips with Lance my first year, and all three of us played together my final year which was also Eric's freshman year.

On one hand, the fact that we all graduated from college wouldn't immediately make sense based on Dad's checkered educational background. On the other hand, his experiences made him value education.

Several years after barely making it through high school, he took a few courses at Washburn University in Topeka, Kansas, and later tried to take classes again at Baker University in Baldwin, Kansas. At the time he started taking classes at Baker, he was working as a clerk in the flight inspection department of General Motors in Fairfax, north of Kansas City; GM was building F-84F jets for the Korean War. He commuted to Fairfax from Topeka for a while, and then moved the family to Liberty, Missouri, to be closer to the job.

Dad worked 3-11:30 p.m. five days a week and commuted the hour each way to and from Baldwin. He took twenty credit hours and made a B average. Son number two, Lance, arrived that year and I was only fifteen months old, so home life got more complicated. Dad had pushed himself to the limit and his health was broken; he spent time in the hospital recovering from exhaustion and pancreatitis. Dad, Mom, and two sons moved back to Topeka and he never went back to college.

Despite all of that, there was never any doubt that the five of us would go to college. From the time I can remember, that was the expectation: prepare in high school and make good grades; and find a way to fund most of college, if not all of it, on our own – through academic scholarships, athletic scholarships, work, grants, loans, or any combination thereof. Dad was not in a position to help much; he did what he could when he could. Mostly he was a cheerleader and provided an inexpensive home base for summer and holiday breaks.

Attend college – it really didn't matter much where, as long as it was accredited and reputable.

Succeed – straight A's weren't expected, thank goodness, but making the honor roll, being involved, and being in leadership roles was important.

Graduate – much to his satisfaction, all five of us did, as have several of his grandchildren.

It was as simple and as complicated as that.

Serious taxi service

I could try to estimate the number of times Dad gave the five of us rides, but it would give me a headache. It know it gave him a headache more than once. When he was in town and on weekends, the rides seemed almost nonstop.

There were summers where the five of us played on at least one baseball team and none of us were old enough to drive. Each team would practice at least once a week and play one or two games a week. Lots of rides.

We all played football on teams before we could drive. Practices and games. Lots of rides.

All five of us had music lessons, played in bands, and/or sang in choirs. There were times when we were involved in church activities. Lots of rides.

Visiting friends and hosting friends, and a few dates. Lots of rides.

In this era before cell phones and texting and call waiting – mixed with our youthful view of time and schedules – Dad had to wait on us more than once. He usually stayed in the car listening to a baseball game on radio or reading for business or pleasure, sure that we would be on time just this once. In the rare cases he had to come to the door to retrieve us, it meant it was going to be an icy cold silent trip home.

(I have often thought that if we had cell phones and call-waiting back then, we could have avoided a lot of angst, many arguments, and multiple groundings.)

For all those years, he patiently and consistently waited and kindly provided a service for us that we didn't fully appreciate until years later.

The art of hosting

Some hosts seem to think the honor of being in their presence should be enough for their guests. The hosts often make an entrance, expect to be the center of attention, and are disappointed if the guests don't treat them with the respect they believe they deserve.

We learned differently. Dad's entire focus was on the guests. He was ready early at home or away, always there to greet each guest as he/she arrived. The food, entertainment, conversation all centered on the guests. Whether any or all of it pleased Dad was not important. It was all tailored to please the guests and to create a nice memory for them.

The ability to host served Dad well in his business and personal life, and we learned by watching.

His town: Kansas City

The Kansas City Chamber of Commerce didn't have any better ambassador than Dad. He knew the town and he loved it. To him, it was the right size, had the right attitude, and was the ideal place to live and work. He loved traveling, but he was always happy to come back home to Kansas City.

He loved being in a town with a Major League Baseball team, initially with the A's and then with the Kansas City Royals. From the time they came to town as an expansion team in 1969, the Royals were his team. He went to as many games as he could afford to either with the family or with clients. In the early years, we listened to Buddy Blattner, Denny Matthews, and Fred White call the games on radio, oftentimes taking a longer route home or sitting in the car in the driveway so we could hear the last innings and final out. In his later years, Dad watched nearly all of the 162 games on television. For Father's Day in 2016, Matt's family purchased a Kansas City Royals World Series Brick in Dad's memory to be placed in the Legacy Plaza in front of Kauffman Stadium. It was a fitting tribute to both Dad and the Royals.

He also loved the Country Club Plaza; a winter print of the Plaza with its holiday lights was one of his prized possessions. He loved shopping there and he loved every Thanksgiving when the Christmas lights were lit for the holidays.

He loved Arthur Bryant's Barbecue and Zeppi's Pizza, which later became Fun House Pizza. He loved Trader Vic's until it closed, hosting many business events there.

He alternately loved and hated the *Kansas City Star*. He loved the Chiefs. He loved the jazz clubs.

He was proud of his town and he taught us to be proud of it, too. In recognition of his love for Kansas City, a month or so after Dad died, Matt scattered some of his ashes in the Plaza, at the Walnut Grove Park near where we grew up at 5022 Reeds Road, and at the pitcher's mound at the baseball field at Rushton Elementary School where we spent many hours practicing and playing while growing up.

Being underestimated is not a bad thing

Throughout his life, Dad was underestimated many times. People underestimated his knowledge, his skill, his preparation, his heart, his perseverance, his athletic ability, his tenacity. He never shied away from it. In fact, he embraced it.

In business, in athletic competition, and in life, he knew that if his competitors underestimated him, they would relax and let their guard down. By the time they realized they had miscalculated, it would be too late. Dad would have the upper hand and be on the way to winning whatever battle it was.

His message to all of us was: be humble, be confident, be yourself, and don't be offended when people underestimate you. Rather, use it as yet another tool to beat the competition. And whatever you do, don't make the same mistake by underestimating your competitors.

911 and emergency rooms

When I was about thirteen months old, I was at the wrong place at the wrong time. I was too young to remember any of this; just going by what I was told.

Mom, very pregnant with Lance, was ironing. I was crawling on the floor. Somehow Mom accidentally hit the ironing board. The iron fell off the board and hit my face on the way to the floor. One cheek was pretty badly burnt. It could have been worse, I'm sure, but it was bad enough.

Paul Kincaid

Since the car was in the repair shop (again), Dad instinctively scooped me up and ran the four blocks to the hospital emergency room. That quick response and the doctor's good work avoided any lasting scars. As a father myself, I can appreciate the instant fear and adrenaline rush that Dad must have experienced. Too bad they didn't have a stop watch on that record-setting quarter-mile dash to the hospital.

That was the first of many times Dad took us to hospitals, doctors, and dentists to help get us put back together. The list is probably what you would expect from five boys playing sports, working manual labor jobs, and taking chances: broken fingers, broken leg, broken ankle, broken nose, broken pelvis, torn ligaments, concussions, dislocated shoulder, dislocated finger, and chipped teeth, to name just a few examples. A couple required ambulance rides. Some required surgery. Others required crutches, casts, splints, and slings. All required patience and money; Dad had more of the former than the latter. The joke was that between Mom and all five of us, we had funded at least one new wing at Shawnee Mission Hospital.

Part of his patience and understanding came from his own experiences. When he was in junior high, he broke his collar bone playing soccer. The principal, J. Otis Scott, carried him to the hospital where they taped it up. He went back to school and rejoined the soccer game. Growing up, he broke teeth and cracked bones often, usually choosing to ignore them and push on.

While I am sure he worried about us, outwardly he took it all in stride. And, he resisted the temptation to ask what in the world we were thinking, which often would have been justified. That was especially true one baseball game in the summer of 1967 when Lance and I, both in our early teens and on the same team, ended up in the hospital emergency room within an hour of each other.

I was pitching and Lance was catching. Lance went for a popup between home plate and first base. Our first baseman, Mike Denny, did the same. They collided at full speed, with Mike's shoulder hitting Lance in the face. His nose and face were swollen to double their normal size almost before he hit the ground. Mom took Lance to the hospital, ultimately to have his broken nose surgically repaired.

My next at-bat was in the bottom of that inning and I was upset about Lance. I was going to take my anger out on the baseball and the other team. I swung hard and missed. But something was wrong. The pain was real and I couldn't walk. I know Dad questioned whether or not I was really hurt; after all, there was no blood or other visible sign of injury. X-rays at the hospital indicated that I had broken a piece of bone off the left side of my pelvis, not exactly a common injury.

There were no cell phones, so the first time Mom knew about my injury was when she came out of the curtained exam area in the emergency room where Lance was being treated and saw me in the wheelchair. My injury required ten days in the hospital in "reverse traction" – head and knees of the bed both elevated – and several weeks on crutches.

We tested our parents' patience that day and in the weeks that followed.

Dad visited us in the hospital, was encouraging with our rehab, and chalked it up to "life in the fast lane." He could not have been more supportive. His only advice – always – was that we needed to drink more milk so our bones would be stronger.

By his example, Dad taught us how to be good patients. Based on all of his experiences, and especially my mom's health issues, Dad hated hospitals and he hated medicine. He was generally leery of doctors, too.

Dad didn't like talking about health. For most of his life, his response to questions about how he was doing was the same: "Just right." In his final couple of years, he grew weary of people asking him some version of, "How do you feel?" In response, Dad starting sticking out his index finger, reaching his arm out, touching you, and saying, "Like this." After you asked that question and got that response a few times, you stopped asking as often. Which, of course, was exactly what Dad had in mind.

On the other hand, Dad also understood that when it was necessary, you had to trust the doctor completely – give in, follow orders, and trust it would work out. He didn't always live up to his own advice.

In the late 1960s, Dad needed to have his gall bladder removed. He had scheduled the surgery, and he and Mom went to the hospital to check in. Uncle Gordon and Aunt Joyce had come from Osawatomie to Kansas City to watch the five of us.

It wasn't long before Dad and Mom were back home. Dad didn't stay for the surgery. He said the waiting line was too long. I assume it was the line to be admitted, but I am not sure; health care was different back then.

About a month later, the pain had escalated, so Dad went back for the surgery. Before going, he checked in with Uncle Gordon. Dad promised he would stay this time. He told Uncle Gordon he only had one concern: "I'm just not sure if they are going to cut or blast."

Dad treated all health care workers with respect. He was polite and funny. He was a "patient patient." He never complained. He never asked for anything unless it was absolutely necessary, sometimes to a fault. For all of those reasons, he was typically identified as the health care workers' best and favorite patient. That was true up to and including his final day.

Exaggerating or bragging?

Dad was proud of our accomplishments. Because he knew it wouldn't be a high priority for us at the time – but also because he knew we would be glad we had them later – he kept multiple scrapbooks for all five of us. Each covered different eras in our lives and were filled with newspaper clippings, game programs, concert programs, photos, athletic letters, speech contest medals, and anything else he thought eventually might have meaning for us. He gave the books to us when we were ready to leave the house and go out on our own. He was right – we were glad to have them.

Sometimes it was embarrassing to listen to Dad tell friends, family, and business associates about our activities, especially athletics. It was not a function of advancing age – he exaggerated early and often. You might consider it the parenting version of NASCAR's "if you ain't cheatin', you ain't tryin' hard enough" – "if you ain't exaggeratin', you ain't braggin' enough."

I would say the exaggeration was consistently in the twenty to twenty-five percent range. If you had six pitching wins in a summer, it would turn into seven or eight. If you hit .300, it would be .360. If you had ten tackles in a game, it would become twelve. And so on.

But one story stands out and gets referenced more often than any other in our family: the time I hit a home run over Earl Butts Dorm. Or at least according to Dad that's what happened.

The game was my last competitive baseball game and it occurred in the summer of 1975 following my senior year at Phillips. Since it was my last game and my last chance, I was allowed to hit for myself late in the game, something I had not done for a couple of years because I pitched and we had the designated hitter. It was my last official at-bat.

The Phillips University baseball field was on campus. It was a small park – straight-away left field fence was about 310 feet. About 100 feet beyond the left field fence were the swimming pool (left field line and left field) and tennis courts (left-center). About fifty feet beyond the pool and courts was Earl Butts Dormitory, which housed about 200 male students. The dorm was constructed with two mirror wings on either side of a central common area and cafeteria. The aerial view would look something like an "H"; from home plate, it looked like the "H" turned on its side. With its design, the structure was about 250 feet wide.

I was a left handed hitter. So, for Dad's story to be true, I would have had to hit the home run over the fence, over the swimming pool and tennis courts, and over both wings of the dorm – some 710 feet…to the opposite field.

The truth is, I did hit a home run to the opposite field – a high fly ball that cleared the fence by about three feet. Had the left fielder not mistimed his jump, he might have caught it.

Now that I see it in writing, I know why Dad exaggerated – his story sounds much better than the truth.

Paul Kincaid

Family first

Growing up in a family of five or more children is different than a family with one or two kids or even four. It just is. Growing up in larger families is like being part of a team, not just having a companion or two.

My brothers and I were best friends growing up. We still are, even though we have our own personalities, different beliefs, and individual styles. When it is all said and done, being brothers transcends everything else. That was Dad's hope and expectation. We knew Dad always had our back and he taught us to do the same for each other.

In public, we always stuck up for each other and were each other's loudest cheerleaders. If someone dared take one of us on, everyone else came to the rescue. That was in public. In private, we would argue and disagree, and take whatever corrective action was appropriate.

Dad made his expectations clear: have the courage to do the right thing, treat people with respect, be polite, have good manners, don't lie, take responsibility for your actions…and, always, put family first. Like most great teachers and coaches, Dad created an atmosphere where we didn't want to disappoint him or let him down. It was a powerful tool and one byproduct was it drastically reduced the need for punishment.

To be good brothers, we learned to be dependable, to have our word be our bond, to root for each other, and to trust and be trusted. We had to learn to be as good as followers as we were as leaders. In the process of becoming good brothers, we also learned how to be good teammates in athletics and good colleagues at work.

Question authority

Dad expected us to respect authority, but also to question it. Even his. When it came to questioning authority, Dad led by example and we didn't need much encouragement to follow his lead.

We didn't question Dad often, but it did happen, especially during our adolescent years, which with five of us lasted a more than a decade. If he ever took offense, he never showed it. And his acceptance of our occasional challenges made our relationship stronger.

In our careers the "question authority" advice was not always welcomed. It was in our DNA and sometimes we just couldn't help ourselves. Most of the time, we were smart enough to question authority in the proper manner at the proper times. But not always.

Las Vegas trips

As we grew up and had our own lives, my brothers and I still made time to be with Dad. We had group breakfasts in Kansas City when our travels took us there. We tried to go to Kansas City Royals games together or watch the games on television. And we went on a two-day fishing trip which we referred to as our "floating picnic" since we were more successful at snacking than catching fish.

But the favorite memories came later in life, as adults, when we were able to take "boys only" trips to Dad's favorite city: Las Vegas. It was one of the highlights of his final ten years.

Growing up, Eric, Kevin, and Matt had all gone to Las Vegas individually with Dad, usually related to his business. And Dad had gotten Lance hooked on Las Vegas; Lance and his wife, Nancy, have gone fairly frequently for many years. Dad also went to Las Vegas with Susan. Each time before he went, he would call and say, "Son, we're going to spend some of your inheritance – we're headed to Las Vegas."

Dad loved the sights and sounds and constant activity of Las Vegas. He played deuces wild video poker and five dollar table Blackjack. He always wanted to see the classic car museum on the top floor of the old Imperial Palace. He loved the buffets, especially in the early days when they were so inexpensive. And he always wanted to stop by the Gamblers General

Store on Main Street so he could stock up on chips and playing cards for his monthly poker games.

Dad had several pieces of advice that he repeated often, including "don't gamble at the airport" and "always bet the maximum." His favorite saying was: "We didn't come here to break even." And, regardless of how it turned out, I guess you could say he always achieved that goal.

Our first boys only trip was in 2006, with all five of us taking Dad for his 75th birthday. We stayed at Treasure Island. Kevin passed away in 2009, and a few years later the four of us decided to revive the tradition with Dad. We went back in 2013 and 2014, staying in different rental houses both times to better accommodate Dad's limited mobility, his use of a wheelchair, and his desire to sleep more upright in a recliner.

We were happy to watch out for him, but not without a fairly constant steam of joking at his expense. He would take it and then return fire.

There are no words to adequately describe the joy it gave Dad to have his grown sons willing to make time to spend with him in his favorite city. These trips are among the final lasting memories we made with Dad.

On our trip in 2014, Dad announced it would be his last trip to Las Vegas. He was right. In late September 2015, about seven weeks after Dad passed away, we returned to keep the tradition alive. While there we sprinkled some of Dad's ashes at Caesar's Palace and the grounds of the chapel where he and Susan were married.

Always choose humor

Dad couldn't help himself. He was just funny. He looked for and saw the humor in everything and he taught us to do the same.

Like the saying goes, you can either laugh or cry. The optimist looks for reasons to laugh, and Dad certainly was an optimist. He chose to laugh – at his own foibles as often as at life and specific situations. He took seriously his role as dad, his commitment to family, his friendships, and his work. But not himself.

Humor can be disarming. It can reassure. It can heal. It can allow you to connect to others in a special way and more quickly. It is often cited as an essential tool to being a great leader. Humor can even make you more attractive, especially to the opposite sex.

Done sincerely and correctly, self-deprecating humor is the best. Being able to laugh at yourself keeps you grounded and helps you deal with your imperfections. If you can't laugh at yourself, then you can't truly enjoy humor. And, you really could not have survived growing up in our family. When any of us showed signs that we could not handle humor, we became a target for a barrage until we responded appropriately.

Dad was able to see the humor in even the most difficult situations. His brand of humor was not like prepared jokes in a stand-up routine. Rather, it was quick-witted humor in response to a situation or moment. Like him, his humor was authentic and spontaneous.

We learned the important difference between humor and sarcasm. Humor makes people laugh easily and freely. Sarcasm can be funny, but it also has an edge, usually has a target, and sometimes can be mean-spirited and even cruel. There are times the line between the two blurs.

As we were growing up, all of us had to endure the usual mean comments from our peers, often about our weight, other physical features, our profuse sweating, or the way we dressed. We never started the verbal sparring, but we were quick to respond and we did so pointedly. We were pretty good at it.

Sometimes, we let that pointed sparring carry over to our home with each other. Fortunately, we outgrew that adolescent stage and found the joy and value in true humor that is laugh-out-loud funny, not a weapon.

For most of his life, Dad had the same dry response when we laughed at his expense: "Very funny."

Paul Kincaid

Embarrassing inspiration

But there was nothing funny or normal about that day in 1962. I was nine and I was so uncontrollably mad I was shaking. I went to sit on Dad's lap in his chair as he requested.

"What's wrong?" Dad asked. "Why are you so mad?"

I gave an explanation, I am sure, but to this day, I don't recall the details. I do remember the punch line, however.

"I am so mad at you I could spit in your face," I said in my rage.

"If that will make you feel better," Dad responded, "go ahead."

And I did. Then I jumped off his lap and ran to my room.

I cannot imagine how badly that made him feel or how mad it made him, even if just for a moment. But there was no spanking, no time out, no retribution of any kind. We never talked about it. Fifty years of father-son life has gone on as if this event never occurred.

I have had plenty of regrettable moments in my life, but this is the one of which I am least proud. Thinking about it makes me feel about as badly as a son can feel. If I could undo it – if I could erase it – I would.

At the same time, Dad inspired me by how he handled it – with understanding and instant forgiveness, all as a young, inexperienced father at age thirty-one.

For me, the inspiration in this embarrassing situation was this: if Dad could respond that way to being spit in the face by his nine-year-old son, there shouldn't be anything I cannot endure as a father to my two kids.

CHAPTER FIVE

Game over

Dad knew the time had come.

On Monday, August 3, 2015, he said his goodbyes.

On Tuesday, August 4, he apologized to Lance and Matt for taking so long to die. Not surprisingly, he repeatedly expressed his frustration with a sports metaphor: "Let's get this f---king game over."

On Wednesday, August 5, he began to fade. He stopped talking around noon. Early that evening, he slipped in and out of consciousness as each individual breath became increasingly more difficult.

Shortly after midnight on Thursday, August 6, he took one last deep breath.

When he said his goodbyes on Monday, he did so in person to Susan; to my brothers Lance and Matt; and to his sister, Jean, and her husband, Jerry, all of whom lived in Kansas City and checked on him routinely.

He called Eric in Dallas. He called a couple of friends – Bob Brunker in Kansas City and Terry Butzirus in Lincoln, Nebraska. And he called me at about four o'clock Monday afternoon.

I was just finishing an eye exam when the call came in. I had been alerted he was making calls, so I wasn't surprised. I knew it was going to be a difficult call, so I let it go to voice mail, finished my exam, and hurried to my car. In the meantime, Matt sent a text asking me to call as soon as I could.

As I began heading home, I listened to the twenty-three second message which I still have saved. In a soft, hoarse voice, Dad said:

> "Hey Paul, I guess I'm going here pretty quick. I just wanted to call and tell you one last time that I love you...love you so much. You've given me a lot of pleasure over the years. Take care of yourself. Please help take care of Susan. Bye-bye."

It had only been in his final few years that he told my brothers and me that he loved us. We always knew it, but he did not say it out loud very often. I credit Susan with encouraging him to verbalize it more to us just as he did to her. Hearing him say it now was emotional.

As the tears welled up and then started to run down my face, I returned the call. Dad answered and repeated his heart-felt message. Choked up, I told him that he had been a great dad and that he had inspired my brothers and me to try to be good dads, too. He said he hoped that was true. I assured him it was. He told me he loved me and I told him I loved him. That was our last conversation.

After I hung up from that Monday call, I called Lance and Matt to see if I should head to Kansas City. The doctors said there was no way to tell how long he had, but there were no signs that death was imminent.

I stayed in touch the rest of Monday and Tuesday. By mid-afternoon Wednesday, the advice was different. Lance and Matt suggested I head to Kansas City as soon as possible, so I started packing. Eric also packed and started to head north from Dallas, planning to arrive in the early morning hours Thursday.

I arrived at Dad's apartment around 10 p.m., joining Lance and Matt who had been there for some time. It was pretty clear Dad was on the home stretch. He was in his recliner, which had been his 24/7 location for several weeks. He hadn't spoken since late afternoon.

Lance, Matt, and I took turns sitting on either side of his recliner holding his hand, rubbing his arm, and talking to him. Susan tried to stay busy at other things, but was always nearby. The Compassionate Care Cardiac Hospice worker sat across the room reading, pausing to listen to Dad's breathing and periodically checking his vital signs.

By the time I arrived, there was no indication that Dad knew what was going on or who was in the room. But he may have. The hospice worker said sometimes dying patients continue to hold on and fight when family members are present. About 11:30 p.m., she offered for us to take a break and promised to call us if something changed. After some discussion – and hesitation – Lance, Matt, and I decided to take her up on her offer.

The worker was right. Within minutes after we left, Dad's breathing became more difficult. She called and we headed back, but he took his last breath just minutes before we got there.

Game over.

I already have been to more funerals than I care to count, but I had not been in the presence of death itself. Matt had been in the hospital room when our Aunt Mary Liz passed away, and Eric had to officially identify our brother, Kevin, when he died of a heart attack in 2009 in Texas. Like them, I know the images, feelings, and sounds will always be fresh in my memory.

In hindsight, I think it helped to have the couple of hours earlier with Dad to prepare for what was about to happen. Those couple of hours reminded us that Dad was not having any fun. Although he never complained, he was in obvious pain and couldn't get comfortable. He had made it clear he was tired of fighting and ready to call it quits.

We called Eric and caught him as he was approaching Oklahoma City. He turned around and headed back to Dallas. Eric had lived away from Kansas City since going to college in 1974, so he and Dad talked at least once every week. Those calls had extra meaning since Eric most closely followed in Dad's career footsteps in advertising sales. Eric had had a long conversation with Dad a few days earlier and said he was at peace with his final goodbye.

Lance, Matt, and I stood outside the apartment in the cool midnight air. We periodically went back into the apartment to check on Susan and to see Dad again. We talked about a lot of things.

We reminded each other of how accurate the Compassionate Care Cardiac Hospice doctors had been in their predictions. The last time he was in the hospital, the doctors determined Dad's congestive heart failure was progressing and terminal. Dad did not want to go to an assisted living facility and he hated hospitals, so he and Susan signed up for cardiac hospice. Under the plan, all heart-related care and end-of-life activities would occur at home. Compassionate Care told us what to expect and the timetable. Being proud sons, we assumed Dad would exceed the norm. He didn't. Their predictions were spot-on.

We talked about how quickly Dad had declined. Six days before he died, I had traveled to Kansas City to watch the Royals game with him on television while Susan had a night off and went out with a friend. Four days before he died, he was the big winner at the monthly poker game with the group he had started more than twenty-five years earlier.

We admired, once again, how he never lost his sense of humor, even in his final days and hours.

A week earlier, he was on the portable toilet near his recliner, which was necessary for the final weeks of his life. Often times, either Matt or Lance had to go to the apartment to assist Dad in that process – sometimes in the middle of the night. With his sedentary state, constipation was an ongoing problem.

On this occasion, Susan asked from across the room: "How are you doing, Leon?" Without hesitating, Dad responded: "Crappy."

The afternoon he passed away, Jean and Jerry called to say they wanted to stop by. By this time Dad was naked, just covered by a sheet in his recliner.

He would periodically and inadvertently push the sheet away, leaving his private parts exposed.

Susan told him, "Leon, Jean and Jerry are coming over. You need to keep the sheet up so you are covered."

To which Dad replied, "Don't worry about it. Jerry will just have to be jealous."

We talked about the coincidence of Dad dying early August 6, less than an hour after Kevin's birthday. After Kevin's memorial service January 20, 2009, I tried to find Dad to see how he was doing. He was standing outside alone on a side porch of the church staring blankly into the cold, dark night. I just stood with him, neither of us speaking. Finally, in a hushed, remorseful voice, he said, "I have never felt this low." Now Kevin's birth date and Dad's final day were within minutes of each other.

Lance, Matt, and I talked about what we needed to accomplish in the coming days to help Susan and live up to Dad's request of us. There was virtually no estate to handle – the little that was left was Susan's. And we talked about how best to fulfill his final wishes, which we reviewed.

In about thirty minutes, the registered nurse arrived to officially pronounce him dead.

In another thirty minutes or so, two mortuary workers arrived to take Dad's body away to be cremated. The three of us and the mortuary staff grabbed the sheet under Dad and lifted him from the recliner onto the gurney.

As we lifted him, Dad's right arm flopped back and over this head. Over the previous couple of years, his shoulders and arms – especially his right shoulder and batting practice pitching arm – had become progressively stiffer, less mobile, and more painful when he tried to move them. Now, the arm flopped backward effortlessly. Dad did not grimace or groan – final evidence that his pain was gone. Matt gently lifted Dad's arm and placed on the gurney next to his side.

They rolled Dad out the door and loaded him into the van. As the van slowly pulled off, I said softly to no one in particular: "So long, Dad. Thanks for everything."

It's personal.....or at least it ought to be

Nothing makes me angrier than listening to a eulogy delivered by someone who didn't know the deceased. No matter how well intentioned, it just doesn't work. It's not hard to tell either. The speaker mispronounces names; uses comments like, "I actually didn't have the pleasure of knowing Mary" or "I learned a lot about Joe last night from the family"; and/or reads from a script more than speaks from the heart.

It is bad enough that a life is reduced to a 400-word obituary and a twenty-minute service. Having an "insert-name-here" canned eulogy delivered by a stranger, clergy or otherwise, is, in my opinion, the ultimate insult.

My aversion to the impersonal eulogy has led me to agree to provide remarks for family members. I spoke at my mom's memorial and at Kevin's service. Based on those, Dad had requested that I tell stories about him as well. Dad also invited my brothers to add stories if they wanted, and he asked that two of his closest friends – Bob Brunker and Terry Butzirus – also make remarks.

In every case, I have found the process of writing the eulogies to be my time to remember, grieve, and begin the healing process. Every time, I cried as I wrote, remembering the good times and regretting the bad – feeling satisfied about what I had done and remorseful about my mistakes and the missed opportunities. I always felt added pressure to do a good job on the eulogies since I also was speaking on behalf of my brothers and other family members. By the time I was done writing the remarks, I was one step closer to acceptance.

Dad was specific in his last requests. In addition to identifying speakers, he did not want a formal funeral; he wanted to be cremated because it cost less; he didn't want to be buried anywhere so no one would feel obligated to visit the grave; and he wanted his ashes scattered at the Johnson County 3&2 Baseball Complex. We were committed to following his wishes.

Later the morning of August 6, after only a couple of hours of restless sleep, Lance, Matt, and I went with Susan to make arrangements with the Cremation Center of Kansas City. Then Matt and I worked on the obituary for the Cremation Center website and the *Kansas City Star*. Lance and Susan helped review the obituary before we submitted it. It struck me that the cost of the cremation ($695) was less than the *Kansas City Star* bill for the obituary to run Saturday, Sunday, and Monday (about $800). As Dad would have said, "Breathtaking."

Over the years, I have helped write many obituaries. My goal always was and is to capture the person's personality in more of a story format than normal. I also feel strongly about including the cause of death since it is one of the first questions people ask. Such was the case with Dad's obituary:

Leon Kincaid

Leon Kincaid, born Everett Leon Kincaid, Jr., 84, died in his home August 6, 2015, of congestive heart failure.

Leon loved Kansas City and had lived in Shawnee Mission since 1961 with the exception of two years in Des Moines, Iowa, in the early 1990s. Leon was born March 22, 1931, in Oklahoma City. His family moved to Topeka in 1944 where he graduated from Topeka High. Leon was a longtime successful advertising salesman for farm publications owned and operated by Harvest Publications, HBJ Publishing, and Farm Progress. He played sports growing up, coached baseball in Johnson County 3&2 for many years, and was a lifelong fan of the Kansas City Royals and Oklahoma Sooners. He loved poker and had helped host a monthly poker group since 1987. He also was known for his sense of humor which he shared generously with his family, friends and clients. With the late Darlene S. Schrader, they had five sons, and he claimed that his "only prideful accomplishment was fathering five wonderful sons."

Leon was preceded in death by his father, Everett L. Kincaid, and stepmother Velma Stevens Kincaid; his mother, Joye Glass Titus, and step-father Jasper Titus; and son Kevin Kincaid. He is survived by his wife of twenty-five years, Susan Willey and step-daughter Kristin Willey of Sioux Falls, South Dakota; sister Jean Caldwell and her husband, Jerry; four sons and their wives: Paul and Janet Kincaid of Springfield, Missouri, Lance and Nancy Kincaid of Lenexa, Eric and Nancy Kincaid of Dallas, Texas, and Matt and Julie Kincaid of Leawood; Kevin's widow, Shelly Kincaid of Switzerland; nine grandchildren; ten great-grandchildren; many cousins, nieces and nephews; three brothers-in-law; and many friends.

Fulfilling his wish, Leon was cremated and his ashes will be scattered in a private family service.

The family is especially thankful to the caregivers of Compassionate Care Cardiac Hospice.

There was an opportunity to leave notes on the site, so my brothers and I posted the first one. One of our goals was to indicate that there would not be a funeral and to explain why. We wanted to supplement what the obituary had said without paying the *Kansas City Star* rate to do so.

Comments on "Leon Kincaid"

Paul, Lance, Eric and Matt Kincaid Say:

Dear family, friends, colleagues:

Dad made it very clear what he wanted and didn't want done when he passed. One thing he did not want was a memorial service. There were lots of reasons for that, including he didn't want friends and family spending a lot of money to attend. Had Susan and the four of us gone against his wishes, we are quite sure he would have found a way to haunt us for a long time. We weren't prepared to take that risk.

Besides, if we had a memorial service, we would have to book the venue for about a month to get through all of the material we had on Dad. They say that a parent's role is "to create memories for their children." If that is true (and we believe it is), then Dad set a standard that will be hard to top.

In lieu of a memorial service, we hope you will take a few minutes to share your thoughts here. The family will appreciate it and it will be therapeutic for all of us.

Dad lived a long life – much longer than he ever thought he would. He lived life to its fullest – he most definitely got his money's worth. Once he decided he was ready and it was time, he passed quickly and without pain. Even so, it is difficult and it will take time to accept.

Dad loved his family and he told them so. He treasured his friends and he was a good friend in return; he never took those relationships for granted. He was liked and respected by an amazingly diverse group of people: family, friends, clients, colleagues, competitors, poker group, former players, neighbors, his sons' friends, coaches, and more. Those relationships were due in large part to his humor and his generosity…but especially his humor.

Throughout his life – and certainly raising five boys – Dad used humor as the antidote to just about every challenge: sickness … injury … embarrassment … grief … despair … anger … surprise … boredom … you name it. He was still making wise cracks in his final days and hours. His caregivers told us how great a patient he was and how funny he was.

We especially liked the words of wisdom Dad shared over the years, some of which we have used throughout our own professional careers. Some of our favorites include: "Money's never an issue – as long as you have some of it." "Never get old – it's not all it's cracked up to be." "There's a fine line between being 'in the groove' and being 'in a rut.'"

If you knew Dad, then you knew he wasn't perfect. But, then, he never claimed to be. Besides, he was too busy being a great dad to his five sons to be perfect. He supported us, he showed up for events, he coached us, he corrected us, and he inspired us to be good dads to our own children.

Paul Kincaid

Most importantly, he gave us the freedom to be ourselves, to find our own way, to goof up and grow up, to be individuals. He was always there for us when we needed him. We will miss him greatly. We know you will, too.

Paul, Lance, Eric and Matt

Scattering the ashes

We waited until Saturday, August 29, more than three weeks after Dad died, to schedule a celebration of his life. Since he didn't want a funeral, there was no time pressure to do something quickly. Plus, the extra time allowed family and friends to schedule their work and travel accordingly. In retrospect, it was helpful to have some time between the two. It was hard enough in late August; I cannot imagine how difficult it would have been two or three days after his death.

About thirty friends and family gathered at Lance and Nancy's home to remember. Lance had made arrangements to scatter the ashes at the 3&2 complex, which was less than ten minutes from their house. There was a baseball tournament that weekend, so we were given an approximate time where we would have ten minutes between games. Apparently, the request was not unique and the staff had a plan they implemented.

We arrived at the baseball complex early. Matt had put the ashes in about 50 small double-handled gift sacks of assorted bright colors. Everyone took one as they gathered behind the fence on the first base side. Family and friends, some of whom hadn't seen each other since the last funeral, visited.

When the game ended, we moved everyone to right field near the foul line and fence. Without prompting, everyone formed a circle. I had the role of leader:

Thanks for coming. After we finish here, we will go back to Lance and Nancy's house for some barbeque and stories.

Having his ashes scattered here was very important to Dad for the three things it symbolized.

First, I am not sure if you knew this or not, but Dad was fairly competitive.

He was competitive in work…play…gambling…driving…all aspects of life. He even took delight in having outlived most of his colleagues and adversaries.

One of the great gifts Dad gave my brothers and me was teaching us how to compete: working hard toward a goal…being tough…being persistent…being relentless…being a great teammate…being humble in victory…and being gracious in defeat. Now that I think of it, Dad never spent much time on the "being gracious in defeat" part of competition.

Dad's love of competition is why we are here.

Second, largely because he craved competition, he loved sports and games.

He loved playing them growing up…and he played them full blast. He was Pete Rose before Pete Rose, sliding head first, running over the catcher blocking home plate. And that was in a church softball game. He would do whatever it took to win.

Dad loved any and all sports and games: football…golf…racquetball…tennis… ping pong…snooker…pool…poker…carom…Yahtzee…backgammon…horse racing…basketball… solitaire…bombardier…dice baseball…you name it. But his favorite of all was baseball. That's why we are here.

Finally, we are here because these fields represent the time he spent with his five sons over so many summers.

For most of the years we played here, Dad was either managing or coaching one or more of our teams. To count the amount of time we spent out here over the years, you would not count hours…but rather weeks and months. If you were counting the number of miles we drove back and forth, it would be in the thousands – I can tell you from experience that, while the number of miles didn't change, the rides home seemed longer when you lost and/or didn't play well. And we would be embarrassed to tell you how many healthy midnight hot dog dinners we ate over those years.

What these fields also represent are the many pepper games at home and the team practices leading up to the games – the team practices were highlighted by batting practice. There is no telling how many thousands of pitches Dad threw for batting practice…how many times he threw until he physically couldn't throw any more. The number of players who benefitted from his batting practice pitching over the years would easily fill a minor league stadium.

And most team practices ended with his signature treat: ice cold Pepsis in glass bottles out of the cooler.

Dad's fond memories of those summers with his sons is why we are here.

Competition. Baseball. Time with his sons. That's what these fields represented to Dad, and that is why he wanted his ashes scattered here. We are happy to fulfill his wish.

You have the bags – the festive colors were inspired by what we found in Dad's sock drawer.

Before we scatter the ashes, a toast.

To Dad/Leon/Grandpa: Thanks for creating so many memories for us. They were fun at the time we were making them and they will keep you in our hearts forever. Here's to you.

Celebrating life

We justified our gathering as a "celebration of life," not a funeral or memorial service. That way we thought we could confidently say we had lived up to Dad's wishes. The truth is, the event, no matter what you called, was important for several family members and friends. They needed closure. That was especially true for his older grandchildren, many of whom were going through this kind of grief for the first time.

So after scattering the ashes at the field, we returned to Lance and Nancy's house to finish our remembrance.

We grew up on Arthur Bryant's Barbecue. It was Dad's favorite and we inherited his taste for it. Bryant's was always a treat, even if you had it several days in a row. We had lots of barbecue there and ready, but it had to wait for a few stories.

We gathered everyone in the open space at the bottom of the stairs, with the fourth step on the stairs becoming our podium. I was the emcee. I paid tribute to Susan, not only for their happy years together, but also for how she had taken care of Dad, especially in his final couple of years.

Then we started the stories. I recalled several, all of which are included in this book. In between, I introduced Bob and Terry to speak. Their comments were different, but had some common themes: Dad's abilities as a salesman, his generosity, his love of life, and, of course, his humor. All three of us struggled to get through our remarks.

As we came to conclusion, Susan surprised all of us by having granddaughter Natalie, Kevin's oldest daughter, read a letter. It was, in essence, Susan's love letter to Dad, remembering their nearly twenty-five years of marriage, the fun they had, and how profoundly she already missed him.

I had prepared a closing, but it didn't seem appropriate after Susan's letter, so I just thanked everyone and invited them to enjoy the barbecue and visit with each other.

Even though I didn't use it, I shared my prepared closing with my brothers. It was our benediction:

Dad was unique – he showed up…he was a doer…he was generous and performed many "random acts of kindness."

He was adventuresome…conservative…opinionated…creative…optimistic…hopeful.

Paul Kincaid

He was extremely funny – he just couldn't help himself…he didn't take himself seriously and he was always willing to laugh at himself…he relied on humor to get through both good times and bad.

He had a laser-sharp wit…he could be disarmingly sarcastic…he could be outrageous… sometimes he was obnoxious…often times he needed to be rated at least "R" if not "X."

He was a loyal and trustworthy friend…and a fierce and feared adversary.

He was competitive and, mostly, a very tough hombre. On the other hand, he was a marshmallow to all kids, but especially his grandkids/great grandkids.

Most of all, he loved his family. He was our biggest fan. He was there whenever any of us needed him. He always had our back.

To my four brothers and me, he was "perfectly imperfect." We experienced and appreciated the total package. He was our hero.

Like all of you, we will miss him a lot. We already do.

Dad's sincere thanks

Dad appreciated those who took time to help him along the way. More importantly, he was good about expressing his appreciation – with notes, cards, emails, phone calls, and public acknowledgments. The following are his tributes to the people who he said contributed to his life and helped him "far more than I deserved." He created this list around 2012 and updated it in early 2015.

―――――――――――――

Five Sons (In age order)

Paul Kincaid – A treasure, one of the best things that has ever happened to me. I take pride in his many accomplishments, his ethical way of life. He has presented me with a nice daughter-in-law and two wonderful grandchildren.

Lance Kincaid – Another one of my major accomplishments. Lance, his wife Nancy, and their two daughters (my granddaughters) and ten great grandchildren are all classy people who live an exemplary life. They give meaning to my life. *(Note: in 2016, another grandchild was added for a total of eleven.)*

Eric Kincaid – My crazy lefthander has made me smile a lot over the years. Love and pride do not really give the total feeling I have for Eric, Nancy, and Allison. They are awesome.

Kevin Kincaid *(Died in 2009 at age forty-nine)* – I miss him, think of him every day. Shelly and the girls are all I have left to remind me of him.

Matt Kincaid – Youngest son has been very close over the years, with us sharing humor as well as personal struggles, etc. He and Julie have two wonderful children whose talents and accomplishments are outstanding. It is a privilege to have his family be part of my family.

Other Children

Kristin V. Willey – Susan's daughter who handles her disability much better than I could.

Bob Brunker – Almost a "sixth son." He and his beautiful family have become close friends after being good clients. He has helped us in many ways, is a generous and high-moral man who I admire greatly. Besides that, he is a good poker player and a great golfer.

Other Family Members (Listed in alphabetical order)

Sandra Stephens Brown – My stepsister who taught me to not trust women in general, her specifically.

Norma Jean Kincaid Crook Caldwell – My loving sister, who has endured me all her life.

Darlene Schrader Kincaid – A beautiful young lady who graced me with marriage, put up with me, presented me with five terrific sons who are the light of my life.

Susan Holdridge Humann Willey Kincaid – A lovely lady whom I called on. She was very upbeat about life, despite being a single mother of a handicapped daughter, she brightened up every room she entered. She became my client, then my friend, then my lover, then my wife. I am beyond fortunate to share my life with her.

Gordon Schrader – A magnificent brother-in-law who was/is my brother in life, who told me when I divorced his sister that "divorce is not a team sport. We will always be friends." He is a giant of a quality person, his family treasured friends.

Eunice Gertrude Joye Glass Kincaid Titus – My mother, who taught me so much, mostly love.

Friends and Business Colleagues (Listed in alphabetical order)

JoAnn Alumbaugh – A beautiful lady who loves ag, was so helpful to me during my Farm Progress years, is still one of my favorite people in the business world.

George Bauer – A small, mean man who pushed me beyond all hesitation I had about being a salesman.

Patty Brown – A dear friend who has for years brighten the darkest of my days just by laughing. A special person.

Mike Buckley – A man I admired who was a musician, a talented ad executive, who became a delightful friend.

Terry Butzirus – One of my dearest friends, a most talented sales executive and golfer. He and Pat have been such good friends I can hardly believe my good fortune. He has been a vocal supporter of me for a long time and it is just his classy way of living that I admire. I am fortunate to have this friendship.

Bob Cain – Such a close friend, a darling man whose humor, love of life, loyalty to our friendship all made my professional life more precious, as it did my personal life.

Hugh Chronister – The most perfect CEO I ever worked for. He helped me financially, business ways, etc.

Ken Constant – A talented man who taught me so much about sales preparation, word selection, how to be classier than I was.

Harvey Crable – My best friend who constantly helped me, taught me so much about selling. A loyal man.

Glenn Danusen – A delightful client and good friend.

Dick Dodderidge – A talented, dear man who took me under his wing and taught me so much about advertising. He and Ann are still good friends.

Bob Edgel – Greatest sales manager I ever met; totally loyal to friends. He tragically committed suicide when several friends lost money from his business.

Walt Eggers – He was creative, successful, and hired good people, most of whom became my good friends.

Paul Fink – Paul was one of my best friends in high school and we later served in the National Guard together. I thought he was so very excellent by all standards that I named my first son after him.

Rod Fletcher – A successful CEO who treated me very well in all ways. He was a class act with a great sense of humor.

Connor Flynn I and II – Classy clients who loved to laugh, were protective of me with their clients. A strong Catholic family, his grandfather, father, and now his son all have run the advertising agency.

Chet Frazier – A huge talent who became CEO of a large ag agency, a loyal friend who helped me get started in ad sales. He had an outstanding sense of humor. He made me a hero buying ads for Purina.

Bob Gage – Skelly Oil executive who taught me a lot.

David Garst – A bombastic CEO who befriended me for years, gave me tons of business, was a superb person to do business with. As with most brilliant people, he was insufferable, but I came to love the man.

Jerry Grittin – Creative, funny, loyal. A wonderful Texan.

Mary Beth Haiar – The Queen of St. Patrick's Day in Sioux Falls. She sent me my first email, was a Godsend to me during some intense business and personal financial struggles. She was struggling with a biker bitch boss, I tried to keep her morale going, we both endured…her better than me. She is also a passionate Chiefs fan – like me – and we have bonded over them and their struggles. Our golf matches were really fun.

Janet Hanf – A dear friend, loyal secretary, who helped guide me through over thirty years of sales efforts.

Larry Harper – A dear man who loved his job as much as I loved mine… and who respected my efforts.

Ken Hickerson – A dear man who has been a loyal friend, an amazing talent, a bright light in my life.

Darrel Holscher – A classy man who shares my conservative political views who has tolerated my emails over the years far beyond what most folks would endure. I admire his very superior intelligence.

Alan Johnson – Farm Progress CEO who was generous, gave me more opportunities than I deserved.

Sheree Johnson – A lovely lady who has been a personal and business friend for more than thirty years. She has endured me and my sales antics far longer than she should have.

Jack Keller – Jack is a great talent, a very likeable guy, a good friend.

Steve Keppy – A personable guy who can make any sourpuss smile – even me!

Joyce Koranda – Another dear lady who worked with Susan, who became a very good friend as well as a very loyal client. She helped my career – as did Susan – far more than I deserved.

Pete Kovac – A client/friend who climbed up from being a junior account executive to being the most powerful advertising agency CEO in Kansas City. Always my friend, always gave me every bit of help he could.

Mick Kreidler – Another very classy professional editor who was at my side when I needed friends when I was stationed in Des Moines. She and JoAnn kept my spirits up through tumultuous times.

Walt Lips – A rascal, but who became a good friend, who helped me have lots and lots of fun in my travels, and was very helpful in my sales efforts.

Franklin "Tud" Love – A gentle boss who showed me so much kindness it influenced how I treated people all my life.

Jerry Lucht – A good boss who helped me extend my sales career further than I thought possible.

Karen McDonald – A dear lady who helped me generously when she could. She made me look good sales-wise.

Frank McGrath – My high school baseball coach, who rescued me from teenage insanity, whose faith in me helped me find better paths in life.

Charles Mead – He and Gracie made my Houston trips joyful.

Dorothy Medlang – A receptionist who was fiercely loyal to me, helped with contacts at her agency beyond the normal scope of expectations.

John Megown – A dear man, a good friend, a shaker and mover in politics who helped me so much in all ways.

Fred Meier – A dear friend who marched the same path in life as I have in many ways, but with undoubtedly better results. He bolstered my morale a lot at times when I needed it. A good man.

Rita Meiners – A fun lady to work with whose loyalty was awesome, as was her sense of humor.

Felix Morris – A darling man I met and worked for in his late years. Generous, fun, loyal.

Kristi Moss – A vice president for media who knows her stuff, was a huge help to me in my sales efforts. She is at the top of her field – media – along with my Susan. I feel fortunate to have her friendship.

Byron Nicedemus – A wild and crazy man who became a close friend.

Nick Nicholson – Pete Kovac's partner, a creative specialist whose humorous artistry still adorns the walls of my office.

Cliff Nothdurft – Another ad agency guy who was generous with time and advice. He died far too young.

Joe Pratt – A dear man whose vision was astounding. He was a shaker and a mover, and I was fortunate to have him as a friend, a client, and a mentor. Truly a class act.

Stan Priske – A wild man, a great friend as well as strong client.

Charlie Quindlen – A bombastic, incredibly good salesman who taught me a lot about sales presentations.

Bill Ransom – Gave me my first job in ag advertising. We were friends for a while, then enemies, then friends again at the end of his rather tragic life.

Chuck Roth – A super sales manager who was immensely helpful with my sales efforts. He made quick decisions, right decisions, was always mindful of what I needed to make sales, was dependable backup.

Charles Rowland – A childhood friend who played, fought, laughed through grade school and teen years. He taught me how to find humor in most all things.

Austin Schnacke – Business friends, personal friends for a while, then the friendship became just a business relationship. We clashed a lot, shared a lot of sales-related adventures, a lot of personal activities.

J. Otis Scott – My grade school principal. A man of dignity and fairness, mixed with sternness when needed.

Dale Sharp – Cadillac/Pontiac dealer in Topeka. Was a dynamic sales giant who pushed me to do well.

Tony Shimkus – Worked on the Purina account, helped me look like a hero constantly, a loyal friend.

John Shull – My junior high school coach who taught me a lot about team involvement. He had faith in me when I did not have much in myself.

Jerry Sleeper – My close friend through high school who always saw the bright side of life even during the many tragedies in his family.

George Smith – An editor who was human, my friend, who did all he could to help me.

Marti Smith – A generous lady who gave me work when I needed it, became a trusted friend, still is a good friend despite the crashing of our business relationship.

Diane Stadlen – A dear lady who was very helpful in my sales career. A classy woman.

"Mouse" Straight – Worked at Spencer Chemical and provided loads of business over the years. A serious drinker who gave me lots of business.

Tom Tiedeman – Tom was the ultimate Irishman – singer, loved to drink and party, was so very sharp about ag media. I was fortunate to be included in his circle of friends.

Bob Unell – He made my Christmas lunches memorable.

Ron Vandiver – My dear friend, a black man who taught me so much about life as well as about business.

Paul Welsh – A client who became a good friend, who has endured my golf game and my personal troubles on the golf course in a classy manner. He wears well as a friend.

Bill Wernimont – A business friend who always had me laughing within minutes of when we would get together anytime. He and his wife Karen were so classy, such great friends.

Don Willenburg – A media director who taught me a lot, had patience with my ignorance.

There are others who have been bright spots in my life. Age is robbing me of the memory of some names, but I have hopefully kept the good things I learned from them.

I invested a lot of time, travel, study of product and people, and kept a core of good humor to sustain my sales efforts. Thanks to all who contributed to this great life. I learned to listen to clients more than talk, which became the foundation of my sales career.

Many others have no doubt played a part in my professional life, and in my personal life. I have been blessed with clients who were loyal, many who became friends, many who became very close to me. I apologize for any who have escaped my memory, which is getting rusty.

Leon Kincaid

Photos of Dad

I always appreciate when memoirs such as this one include photographs. They help provide context, help put faces with names, and help provide some sense of the changes over time.

On the following pages are thirteen representative photos to illustrate Dad's story. They include photos of many of the key individuals named in the book. I hope they add value to the reader.

My apologies to anyone who was left out. Obviously there are scores and scores of photos that I did not have space to include.

This was Dad in 1943 at age twelve, the same year his parents got divorced. It was traumatic for him. He wandered the Oklahoma cotton fields aimlessly for two days after his aunt gave him the news. That was the main reason he waited until he was fifty-nine to divorce Mom, after all five of us were grown and on our own.

Dad, circa 1950, at age nineteen, shortly before he married our mom, Darlene Schrader. Beginning in 1952, Dad would father five boys in nine years. When people showed their shock at the number and frequency, Dad always had the same response: "We had five sons and then we found out what caused that and stopped." Since people laughed, he repeated it again and again.

This is Dad's mother/our grandmother, Joye Titus, and his stepfather/our grandfather, Jasper "Jap" Titus, circa 1960, when they were in their mid to late fifties. They moved from Oklahoma City to Topeka in 1944 when Dad was thirteen. In the early 1960s, they moved to Mobile, Alabama, where they lived until they passed away, Jap in 1974 at age sixty-nine and Grandma in 1982 at age seventy-two. Dad was close to his mom – while they rarely saw each other, they talked often and wrote regular letters to each other.

This was Dad's father/our grandfather, Everett Leon Kincaid, Sr., and his stepmother/our grandmother, Velma Stevens Kincaid, in 1986 when they were both in their early eighties. Even then they were still running a lawn care business from their home on Lake Texoma in Oklahoma. As a result of his troubled relationship with his own father, Dad vowed to be an involved and good dad to my brothers and me. *(Used with permission. ©Lifetouch Inc. Photography for a Lifetime)*

This family photo was taken on November 8, 1975, in Enid, Oklahoma, at Janet's and my wedding. Back row (left-right): brother Lance and his wife Nancy, who were married in 1973; brother Matt; and brother Eric. Front row (left-right): brother Kevin; Janet and me; and Mom and Dad. Lance was best man, Kevin sang "The Wedding Song (There Is Love)," and Eric and Matt served as ushers. The five of us ranged in age from fourteen to twenty-three, Mom was twenty-two days short of her forty-third birthday, and Dad was forty-four. (*Used with permission. Photo by Lynn Smith/Tintype Studio, Enid, Oklahoma*)

Nearly forty years after our wedding, this photo was taken on March 28, 2015, in Springfield, Missouri, at the wedding of Janet's and my son, Brian, to Danielle Kerckhoff. It was the last family photo in which Dad appeared. Back row (left-right): Jerry and Jean Caldwell, Dad's sister and husband; Gordon and Joyce Schrader, Dad's brother-in-law and wife; Nancy and Eric Kincaid; and Matt Kincaid. Front row (left-right): Janet and me; Danielle and Brian; Jennifer Kincaid, Janet's and my daughter; Natalie Kincaid Mullen, Kevin's oldest daughter; Nancy and Lance Kincaid; and Dad in front. Our ages ranged from fifty-three to sixty-two, and Dad had just turned eighty-two on March 22. (Used with permission. Photo by Katie Day/Katie Day Photography, Springfield, Missouri)

Dad married Susan Willey on April 19, 1991, in Las Vegas, It was their favorite city to visit and they did so as often as they could. They were married nearly twenty-five years. In total, Dad was married nearly sixty-three of his eighty-four and a half years.

Dad was close to his sister/our aunt, Jean Caldwell, who was two years younger than Dad. When Aunt Jean's first husband, Richard Crook, died of a heart attack, Dad began weekly calls to Aunt Jean. At Aunt Jean's request, the calls continued even after she married Jerry Caldwell. Dad called every Thursday at 8 a.m. starting in November 2001 and continuing nearly fourteen years until Dad's death in August 2015. When Dad talked to Aunt Jean on Monday, August 3, 2015, he told her: "When the phone rings this Thursday morning, don't answer it." The phone did ring Thursday morning, August 6. Aunt Jean did answer it. It was Nancy Kincaid calling to tell her that Dad had passed away a little after midnight.

Dad and his brother-in-law/our uncle, Gordon Schrader, shown here in March 2011, referred to each other as "brothers in life." Uncle Gordon, eight years younger than Dad, was the long-time city manager of Osawatomie, Kansas, and a successful Shelter Insurance agent after that. He also was our adviser on a string of used cars my brothers and I purchased from Osawatomie dealers. Over the years, Uncle Gordon helped Dad and Mom whenever and however he could. When Dad and Mom divorced, Uncle Gordon told Dad, "Divorce is not a team sport. We will always be friends." And they were.

Dad started his monthly poker group in 1987, hosting the majority of the games at his home. Some twenty-eight years later, on Sunday, August 2, 2015, four days before he died, Dad was the big winner in his final game with the group. This photo, circa 1996, includes most of the regulars. Back (left-right): Bob Brunker, Kevin Kincaid, Matt Kincaid, Tommy Martinez, and Swede Beckstrom. Seated (left-right): Cecil Little, Dad, Chuck Weber, and Fred Meier. Dad referred to Bob as his "sixth son." What began as a business relationship between Dad and Bob developed into a deep friendship between Dad and Susan and Bob and his family. Over the years, Bob did many things to help Dad and Susan. Bob was one of the people Dad asked to speak at his celebration of life. Swede was Dad and Susan's next door neighbor for several years and close friends for many more years. Fred Meier, a banker most of his career, was one of Dad's long-time friends. They first met when Fred and Dad coached the same baseball team, both with two sons on it. They took some trips together, visited each other when the other was ill or in the hospital, and supported each other through difficult times. For many years, they had a tradition of Christmas shopping together in the Country Club Plaza.

One of Dad's closest professional friends was Bob Cain, shown here with Dad in our house in 1969 during one of Bob's visits to Kansas City. Bob was located in the company's Chicago office, and they worked together for many years. One of the main clients they teamed up on was John Deere. They also met in and spent a lot of time calling on and entertaining clients in St. Louis. Bob had a great sense of humor and a distinctive laugh, which made him a perfect match with Dad. In fact, in this photo they appear ready to get into mischief.

Terry and Pat Butzirus (left), who lived in Nebraska, went to dinner in Las Vegas with Susan and Dad, circa 1995. They were there for a Farm Progress sales meeting where Dad received the "Salesman of the Year" award. The four developed a holiday tradition – for nine years, from 2006-15, Terry and Pat spent New Year's Eve in Kansas City with Dad and Susan. Dad's relationship with Terry began through work and golf outings, developed into Dad being Terry's mentor, and ultimately they became best friends. Every day from January 5, 2015, when Dad went to the hospital with a bleeding ulcer, until August 6, 2015, the day Dad died, Terry called Dad to check on him. Two hundred fourteen days straight and Terry didn't miss a single one. At Dad's request, Terry made remarks at the celebration of life.

For Father's Day 2016, Matt's family purchased this brick to be placed in the Kansas City Royals' Legacy Plaza at Kauffman Stadium. It was a fitting and lasting tribute. Dad loved the Royals and he loved baseball. For him, baseball represented competition and the time he spent with his five sons over many years.

About the author

During his career and life, Paul Kincaid has written hundreds of thousands of words. All nonfiction, they have ranged from news and feature releases, to stories and columns in high school and college newspapers and magazines, to long-range plans for universities and organizations, to speeches and testimony for CEOs and board members, to scripts and PowerPoint presentations, to briefing sheets for state and national elected officials and donors, to freelance articles, to the monthly Lions Club newsletter, to personal letters to family and friends, to family Christmas letters. This, however, is his first book.

Through his life and work, Kincaid and his brothers have used the lessons their dad taught them. For example, during budget development discussions, Kincaid often uses his dad's saying, "Money is never an issue, as long as you have some of it." To be distinctive, Kincaid tips hotel housekeepers with gold dollar coins instead of paper dollars. And Kincaid looks for memorable uses of language: "hard frost" instead of "freeze" when describing reduced hiring, and has wondered about using the term "entremanure" when talking about an agriculture-related entrepreneur.

In his personal life, Kincaid has shared his dad's lessons with his own two children – teaching them how to drive, attending their events, and helping them understand the power of humor. Kincaid attributes his punctuality, persistence, work ethic, love of baseball, and consistency largely to the example his dad set.

Perhaps most importantly, with age Kincaid has come to realize how vital it is for young adults – especially adolescent males – to have positive role models with whom they can identify. This was especially driven home in his work as executive director for Jobs for America's Graduates in Missouri.

JAG is a national program that targets high school students who have potential, but who are, for a variety of reasons, at risk for not graduating from high school. JAG's goal is to ensure the students graduate from high school and succeed afterward. Many JAG students grow up in environments that include poverty and broken families, and many do not have positive male role models in their lives. What JAG students want most are authentic examples of those who have stumbled and fallen, but gotten back up again. They want to hear how those individuals overcame failures, persevered, and succeeded, both in their careers and in their lives.

"A lot of JAG students and other young people do not have a dad like ours," says Kincaid. "My hope is that I have told his true story well enough that readers will be inspired just as my brothers and I were. At its core, it is a story about choosing to be inspired by your own challenges, rather than being defined by them; about choosing to be positive; and about always finding humor, even in the darkest moments."

Kincaid was born in Topeka, Kansas, in 1952, the oldest of five boys. In 1961, the family moved to Mission, Kansas, a suburb of Kansas City, where he and his brothers were raised.

He graduated from Shawnee Mission North High School in 1970, and then embarked on what he calls the "five year, three school" plan. He attended College of Emporia (Kansas) in 1970-71, Kansas State University from 1971-73, and Phillips University (Enid, Oklahoma) in 1973-75.

"College of Emporia and Phillips, both small liberal arts universities, no longer exist, so I tell my friends at K-State, 'you better watch out,'" jokes Kincaid.

For thirty-nine years, Kincaid worked in public relations, marketing, and governmental relations at three universities in the Midwest: Phillips (1975-76); Emporia State University in Kansas (1976-86); and Missouri State University (formerly Southwest Missouri State University) in Springfield (1986-2014). He retired from Missouri State in 2014 as chief of staff to the president and assistant to the president for university relations and governmental relations.

The day after retiring from Missouri State in the fall of 2014, he began serving clients through his consulting company, Kincaid Communications, LLC. Kincaid Communications provides counseling in public relations, marketing, crisis communications, and governmental relations primarily to schools and nonprofit organizations. The website is: www.KincaidCommunications.com

During his career, he has been active with various professional organizations, including the Public Relations Society of America (accredited and member of the College of Fellows) and the Council for the Advancement and Support of Education (CASE). Over the years, he received many national and regional awards for his work and distinguished service.

Competitive athletics played a major role in Kincaid's life and personal development, and they have proven to be a great source of true, funny, and inspiring stories.

Kincaid played football through high school and his freshman year in college. The highlight of his football career was playing on the 1969 Shawnee Mission North High School team that was the first to win the state championship through a playoff system. That year included the infamous 1-0 semifinal win, the point being awarded based on penetration after a scoreless four quarters.

He played baseball through college. In 1971, he was 11-1 as a pitcher for the Olathe Rebels American Legion team. In 1972, at age eighteen, he helped Guy's win twelve straight games on the way to the Ban Johnson championship and then the Kansas City championship. Kincaid was the closer for the final six games of the streak – three-game best of five playoff sweeps of Feld and then Butternut. In 1975, Kincaid had a 9-2 record as a starting pitcher to help the Phillips University team earn one of eight spots in the small college world series.

Kincaid has been married to Janet (Wilenzick) since 1975. Since 1986, they have lived in Springfield, Missouri, where their two grown children also live: daughter Jennifer, and son Brian and his wife, Danielle.

www.ingramcontent.com/pod-product-compliance
Lightning Source LLC
Chambersburg PA
CBHW020007050426
42450CB00005B/357